CONVERSATIONAL KOREAN DIALOGUES

Over 100 Korean Conversations and Short Stories

Conversational Korean Dual Language Books

www.LingoMastery.com

978-1-951949-29-7

CONTENTS

INTRODUCTION

So, you want to learn Korean, beloved reader? Excellent — if you've purchased this book then you're already well on your way to doing so. Korean is the official language in Korea. It is used by 45 million people in South Korea and 23 million in North Korea; it is also spoken among several million Koreans living in other countries such as the United States, China, Japan, Russia, and Central Asia. The number of Korean learners is rapidly spreading over the world with the increase in the global popularity of Korean culture and future value including business opportunities. With this book you can make this number bigger by at least one point!

And most importantly, you can do it in a fun and really efficient way. If there's something we know for sure after years in the language learning world, it is that many students choose — or are provided with — the wrong means of study, with professors giving them boring textbooks full of rules they'll never learn or need in a real world situation; while others may overwhelm them with reading material that only serves to make them feel uncomfortable and doubtful of their own skills and level as a Korean learner.

Our goal with this book is to allow you, the reader, to encounter useful, entertaining conversations that adapt very well into dozens of real life situations that you can and certainly *will* encounter in the Korean-speaking world, giving you a chance to fend for yourself when you come across them!

Vocabulary is crucial to learning *any* new language, and the conversations in this book will *guarantee* you pick up plenty of it and watch how it is applied to real life.

What this book is about and how it works:

This book will ensure you practice your conversational skills in Korean through the use of **one hundred and five examples of conversations,** written in both Korean *and* English to allow you to fully understand what's going on in each and every one of them.

Each new chapter is an entirely new, fresh conversation between two people of an everyday situation you may tackle sooner or later. You'll be able to observe how to handle yourself when it comes to checking in at a hotel, asking for directions, meeting an old friend or ordering food at a restaurant, among many others.

If you want to ensure proper understanding of the story, we recommend you read the story in both languages and follow the narrative in a way that gives you the chance to cross-reference what's going on in Korean by checking out the story in clear, concise English.

How was this book created?

The dialogues you'll find inside is the result of collaboration between both English and Korean native speakers. Once written in natural English the stories were translated into Korean and we feel it crucial to give a brief explanation of how it was done.

Since we want you to sound natural, we avoided a word for word translation, so you may come across situations when

- Translations are shorter or longer than the original;
- Some translations are descriptive. For example, there's no way in Korean to say "a red-eye flight" in two words;
- One and the same word is translated differently in different sentences.

For this reason, it might be a good idea to learn whole phrases sometimes, rather than separate words.

So, wake up your inner linguist, analyze, make your own discoveries and get amazed at how different languages work!

Now you know what it is the book will provide you... what are the best ways to use it?

Tips and recommendations for readers of Conversational Korean Dialogues:

This book is certainly easy to pick up and use as many times as you need to, but there are effective ways of applying it to your learning that will get the most out of it. Remember, being effective will not only increase the amount you learn, but also decrease the time you need to spend on doing so!

So, what should you do to improve your learning with **Conversational Korean Dialogues?**

Well, you can always:

1. Roleplay these conversations, whether it's alone or with a friend — Pretending to actually setting up a bank account with a friend may actually do much more for your knowledge of Korean than any lesson will. This book provides you with plenty of material so go ahead and act! Your pronunciation, fluency and confidence will all benefit from it!
2. Look up the words you don't understand — there will always be vocabulary and specific terms you may not get and which aren't translated exactly word-for-word (for our purposes of making the conversation realistic in both languages), so you may need a dictionary. Don't feel upset or ashamed of jotting down those words you don't understand for a quick search on the internet later on!
3. Make your own conversations! — Once you're done with this book, pick any conversation from the hundred and five examples you have and adapt it to your own version. Why not make it so that the receptionist of the hotel didn't have rooms? Or maybe the friends meeting each other weren't so friendly, eh? Find something you like and create something new!
4. Don't be afraid to look for more conversations once you've finished reading and practicing with this book — Only through practice can you reach perfection, or at least as closest as you can get to it!

Well that's all we had to tell you, reader. Now go ahead and show the world you can handle anything! Work hard and keep it up, and before long you'll breeze past any Korean lesson.

Believe in yourself, it's all you need to achieve even the impossible!

FREE BOOK!

Free Book Reveals the 6 Step Blueprint That Took Students
from Language Learners to Fluent in 3 Months

One last thing before we start. If you haven't already, head over to **LingoMastery.com/hacks** and grab a copy of our free Lingo Hacks book that will teach you the important secrets that you need to know to become fluent in a language as fast as possible. Again, you can find the free book over at **LingoMastery.com/hacks**.

Now, without further ado, enjoy these Korean conversations.
Good luck, reader!

1

저녁 식사 주문하기

-

ORDERING DINNER (A1)

웨이터: 안녕하세요?

아미라: 안녕하세요?

웨이터: 음료는 무엇으로 하시겠습니까?

아미라: 그냥 물 주세요.

웨이터: 알겠습니다. 메뉴 여기 있습니다. 물은 곧 가져다 드리겠습니다.

아미라: 감사합니다.

웨이터: 물 여기 있습니다. 주문하시겠습니까?

아미라: 아니요, 아직 시간이 좀 더 필요해요.

웨이터: 괜찮습니다. 천천히 주문하세요.

(삼 분 후...)

웨이터: 시간이 더 필요하신가요?

아미라: 아니요, 주문할게요.

웨이터: 좋습니다. 어떤 것으로 하시겠습니까?

아미라: 치킨을 곁들인 어린 양배추 샐러드 주시겠어요?

웨이터: 물론이죠. 샐러드는 수프도 함께 나옵니다. 수프는 크림 토마토와 미네스트론 중에 어떤 걸로 하시겠습니까?

아미라: 음, 크림 토마토로 주세요.

웨이터: 좋은 선택이십니다. 더 필요한 것 있으세요?

아미라: 아니요, 그게 다예요.

웨이터: 좋습니다!

(5 분 후...)

웨이터: 자, 여기 수프와 샐러드 드리겠습니다.

아미라: 감사합니다.

웨이터: 천만에요. 더 필요한 것이 있으시면 저한테 알려주세요.

아미라: 알겠습니다.

(15 분 후...)

웨이터: 식사는 다 하셨습니까?

아미라: 네!

웨이터: 디저트 메뉴를 보시겠습니까?

아미라: 아니요. 감사합니다. 계산서 좀 부탁해요.

웨이터: 물론이죠. 여기 있습니다.

아미라: 감사합니다!

ORDERING DINNER

Waiter: Hi, how are you?

Amira: I'm good, thanks. How are you?

Waiter: I'm great. Thanks for asking. What would you like to drink?

Amira: Just water, please.

Waiter: Okay. Here is the menu. I'll be right back with your water.

Amira: Thanks.

Waiter: Here you go. Are you ready to order?

Amira: No, I need a couple more minutes.

Waiter: No problem. Take your time.

(Three minutes later...)

Waiter: Do you need more time?

Amira: No, I'm ready.

Waiter: Perfect. What would you like?

Amira: Can I have the spring greens salad with chicken?

Waiter: Sure. The salad comes with a soup. Would you like creamy tomato or minestrone?

Amira: Umm, creamy tomato.

Waiter: Good choice. Would you like anything else?

Amira: No, that's it.

Waiter: Great!

(Five minutes later...)

Waiter: All right, here is your soup and salad.

Amira: Thank you.

Waiter: No problem. Let me know if you need anything else.

Amira: Okay.

(Fifteen minutes later...)

Waiter: Are you done with your meal?

Amira: Yep!

Waiter: Would you like to see the dessert menu?

Amira: No, thanks. Just the check, please.

Waiter: Of course. Here it is.

Amira: Thank you!

2

아이스크림 맛
-
ICE CREAM FLAVORS (A1)

제리: 안녕하세요, 어서 오세요!

로빈: 안녕하세요.

제리: 아이스크림 시식 해보시겠어요?

로빈: 네, 그런데 어떤 맛을 시식해야 할지 모르겠어요.

제리: 선호하시는 아이스크림 맛이 있나요?

로빈: 네, 초콜릿, 딸기, 바닐라 맛을 좋아해요.

제리: 초콜릿, 딸기, 바닐라 아이스크림을 맛보시겠어요?

로빈: 네. 감사합니다!

제리: 알겠습니다. 여기 초콜릿 아이스크림입니다.

로빈: 감사합니다.

제리: 어떠세요?

로빈: 너무 단 것 같아요. 바닐라 아이스크림을 맛볼 수 있을까요?

제리: 물론이죠. 여기 있습니다.

로빈: 감사합니다.

제리: 바닐라 아이스크림 맛있나요?

로빈: 네. 초콜릿보다 더 좋아요.

제리: 딸기 아이스크림을 맛보시겠어요?

로빈: 네, 그럴게요. 감사합니다.

제리: 여기 있습니다. 딸기 맛은 저희 고객들이 가장 좋아하는 맛이에요.

로빈: 음! 이거 맛있네요!

제리: 다행이네요! 어떤 맛으로 하시겠어요?

로빈: 딸기 맛으로 할게요.

제리: 콘이나 컵 중에 어떤 걸로 하시겠어요?

로빈: 콘으로 할게요. 얼마예요?

제리: 삼 달러 오십 센트 입니다.

로빈: 여기 있습니다.

제리: 감사합니다. 맛있게 드세요!

ICE CREAM FLAVORS

Jerry: Hello and welcome!

Robin: Hi.

Jerry: Would you like to try some ice cream?

Robin: Yes, but I don't know which one to get.

Jerry: Do you have a favorite ice cream flavor?

Robin: Yes, I do. I like chocolate, strawberry, and vanilla.

Jerry: Would you like to taste our chocolate, strawberry, and vanilla ice creams?

Robin: Yes, please. Thank you!

Jerry: Okay. Here is the chocolate one.

Robin: Thank you.

Jerry: What do you think?

Robin: I think it's too sweet. May I try the vanilla next?

Jerry: Sure. Here you go.

Robin: Thank you.

Jerry: Do you like the vanilla?

Robin: Yes. I like it more than the chocolate.

Jerry: Would you like to try the strawberry ice cream?

Robin: Yes, I would. Thank you.

Jerry: Here you go. The strawberry flavor is a favorite with our customers.

Robin: Mmm! This one is delicious!

Jerry: Great! Which ice cream would you like?

Robin: I will take the strawberry flavor, please.

Jerry: Would you like a cone or a cup?

Robin: I will have a cone, please. How much is it?

Jerry: That'll be $3.50.

Robin: Here you go.

Jerry: Thank you. Enjoy!

3

새 차 고르기

-

CHOOSING A NEW CAR (A1)

닉: 우리 새 차가 필요해.

안드레아: 나도 같은 생각이야. 어떤 차 생각해?

닉: 싸지만 믿을 수 있는 거로.

안드레아: 맞아. 인터넷에서 찾아보자.

닉: 좋은 생각이야. 이거 봐. 사천 달러에 주행 거리가 만 마일 정도밖에 안돼.

안드레아: 음… 너무 싸다. 아마 차에 문제가 있는 게 아닐까?

닉: 아마 그럴지도 몰라. 계속 찾아보자.

안드레아: 여기 다른 게 있어. 이 차는 주행 거리 육만 칠천 마일에 삼천오백 달러야. 괜찮은데.

닉: 응, 그렇네. 차 문이 2 개야 아니면 4 개야?

안드레아: 4 개야.

닉: 몇 년식이야?

안드레아: 이천십 년식이야.

닉: 그렇게 오래되지는 않았네.

안드레아: 응, 오래되지는 않았어.

닉: 무슨 색이야?

안드레아: 은색.

닉: 오, 좋은 색이네. 그 차를 우리 목록에 추가하자.

안드레아: 좋아. 그리고 여기 다른 차가 있어. 이천칠백 달러고 주행 거리가 십만 천 마일이야.

닉: 마일 수가 너무 많은데.

안드레아: 응. 그런데 이 회사 차는 오래가.

닉: 맞아. 차 상태는 좋아?

안드레아: 뒤범퍼가 약간 패어 있는데 그거 말고는 다 괜찮아 보여.

닉: 좋아. 그것도 우리 후보목록에 추가하자.

안드레아: 좋은 생각이야.

CHOOSING A NEW CAR

Nick: We need a new car.

Andrea: I agree. What kind of car?

Nick: Something cheap but reliable.

Andrea: Yeah. Let's look online.

Nick: Good idea. Look at this one. It's $4,000 and it only has ten thousand miles on it.

Andrea: Hmm… that's so cheap. Maybe the car has a problem?

Nick: Maybe. Let's keep looking.

Andrea: Here is another option. This car is $3,500 with sixty-seven thousand miles. That's pretty good.

Nick: Yeah, that is. Is it a two-door or four-door?

Andrea: It's a four-door.

Nick: What year is it?

Andrea: It's a 2010.

Nick: That's not too old.

Andrea: No, it's not.

Nick: What color is it?

Andrea: Silver.

Nick: Oh, that's a good color. Let's add that car to our list.

Andrea: Okay. And here's another car. It's $2,700 and it has 101,000 miles.

Nick: That's a lot of miles.

Andrea: Yes, but cars from this company last a long time.

Nick: That's true. Is the car in good condition?

Andrea: There is a small dent on the back bumper. But everything else looks good.

Nick: All right, let's add that to our list, too.

Andrea: Sounds good.

4

새끼 고양이를 발견했어

-

I FOUND A KITTEN (A1)

앤디: 미라야, 이거봐!

미라: 뭐?

앤디: 여기 와서 이걸 봐봐!

미라: 뭘 찾았는데?

앤디: 새끼 고양이야!

미라: 아이고, 귀여워라! 어미는 어디 있지?

앤디: 모르겠어. 얘 엄청 작다.

미라: 가여운 것! 얘네 어미를 찾아보자.

앤디: 좋아. 내가 고양이를 안을 테니 주변을 살펴보자.

미라: 알았어. 네가 저쪽을 살피고, 내가 이쪽을 살펴볼게. 15 분 후에 여기서 만나자.

앤디: 좋은 생각이야.

(15 분 후...)

미라: 얘네 어미를 찾았어?

앤디: 아니. 너는 찾았어?

미라: 아니. "길 잃은 새끼 고양이" 알림판을 만들어서 근처에 붙여야겠어.

앤디: 응. 네가 글씨 잘쓰잖아. 네가 할래?

미라: 그래.

앤디: 새끼 고양이를 잃어버린 사람이 있는지 SNS 에 알아볼게.

미라: 그럼 나는 표지판을 만들기 시작할게!

앤디: 우리가 이 새끼 고양이 집을 찾으면 좋겠어! 만약에 못

찾는다면, 얘를 시내 동물보호소에 데려가면 될 것 같아.

미라: 맞아! 그러면 얘는 좋은 가정으로 가게 될 거야. 그리고 그들이 내 이름을 따서 "미라"라고 얘 이름을 붙이면 좋겠어.

앤디: 하하. 아마도 그렇게 할거야!

I FOUND A KITTEN

Andy: Mira, look!

Mira: What?

Andy: Come over here and look at this!

Mira: What did you find?

Andy: It's a kitten!

Mira: Oh my gosh! It's adorable! Where is its mom?

Andy: I don't know. It's so tiny.

Mira: Poor thing! Let's look for its mother.

Andy: Okay. I will hold it and we can look around the area.

Mira: All right. You walk that way and I will walk this way. Let's meet back here in fifteen minutes.

Andy: Good idea.

(Fifteen minutes later...)

Mira: Did you find its mother?

Andy: No. Did you?

Mira: No. We should make "lost kitten" signs and put them up in the neighborhood.

Andy: Yeah. You have good handwriting. Do you want to do that?

Mira: Sure.

Andy: I will check social media to see if anyone has lost a kitten.

Mira: And I'll start making signs!

Andy: I hope we find this kitten's home! If we don't find it, we can take her to the animal adoption center downtown.

Mira: Yes! Then she will find a good home. I hope they name her "Mira" after me.

Andy: Ha ha. Maybe they will!

5

최고의 피자
-
THE BEST PIZZA (A1)

라파엘라: 우리가 뉴욕에 있다니 믿기지 않아!

미키: 맞아!

라파엘라: 뉴욕을 돌아보게 되어 너무 신나!

미키: 나도 그래. 나는 지금 너무 행복해.

라파엘라: 그래서 넌 먼저 뭐하고 싶어?

미키: 나는 너무 배고파. 우리 뭐 좀 먹을까?

라파엘라: 좋은 생각이야! 뭐 먹고 싶어?

미키: 뉴욕에 왔으니까 피자를 먹어야 해!

라파엘라: 뉴욕에 최고의 피자가 있다고 들었어.

미키: 나도 들었어. 건너편에 있는 식당에 가자.

라파엘라: 벌써 피자 냄새가 나!

미키: 어떤 피자를 주문해야 할까?

라파엘라: 치즈 피자가 맛있어 보여.

미키: 나도 그렇게 생각해. 너는 뭐 주문할거야?

라파엘라: 난 페퍼로니 피자를 주문할 거야.

미키: 몇 개 주문할까?

라파엘라: 치즈 피자 두 조각이랑 페퍼로니 피자 두 조각 주문하자.

미키: 좋은 생각이야! 치즈 피자랑 페퍼로니 파자 둘 다 먹어볼 수 있겠다.

라파엘라: 봐! 우리가 주문한 음식이 나왔어.

미키: 지금 하나 먹어볼래.

라파엘라: 어때?

미키: 이 피자 맛있다!

라파엘라: 와, 이거 진짜 맛있다!

미키: 내가 먹어 본 피자 중에 최고인 것 같아!

라파엘라: 나도 그렇게 생각해! 난 이 피자가 너무 좋아!

THE BEST PIZZA

Rafaella: I can't believe we are here in New York City!

Mikey: I know!

Rafaella: I am so excited to explore this city!

Mikey: Me too. I'm very happy right now.

Rafaella: So, what would you like to do first?

Mikey: I'm very hungry. Should we get food?

Rafaella: That is a great idea! What do you want to eat?

Mikey: We are in New York so we should get pizza!

Rafaella: I heard New York has the best pizza.

Mikey: I heard that too. Let's go to the restaurant across the street.

Rafaella: I can smell the pizza already!

Mikey: Which one should I order?

Rafaella: I think the cheese pizza looks good.

Mikey: I think so, too. What are you going to get?

Rafaella: I will get the pepperoni pizza.

Mikey: How many should we get?

Rafaella: Let's get two slices of the cheese pizza and two slices of the pepperoni pizza.

Mikey: Good idea! We can both try a cheese pizza and a pepperoni pizza.

Rafaella: Look! Our order is ready.

Mikey: I'm going to try one now.

Rafaella: How is it?

Mikey: This pizza is delicious!

Rafaella: Wow, this is amazing!

Mikey: I think this is the best pizza I've ever had!

Rafaella: I think so, too! I love this pizza!

6

새 룸메이트
-
NEW ROOMMATE (A1)

리즈: 안녕, 데릭!

데릭: 안녕, 리즈! 어떻게 지내?

리즈: 잘 지내. 근데 스트레스를 조금 받고 있어.

데릭: 왜?

리즈: 새 룸메이트를 급히 찾아야 해.

데릭: 사라 이사 갔어?

리즈: 응. 로스앤젤레스에서 취직했어.

데릭: 와, 잘됐네! 걔한테 말이지...

리즈: 응, 걔한테는 말이지! 사라는 완벽한 룸메이트였어. 걔만큼 좋은 룸메이트를 찾을 수 있을지 모르겠어.

데릭: 글쎄, 아마 완벽한 룸메이트는 못찾겠지만 좋은 사람은 찾을 수 있을 거야!

리즈: 그러길 바래. 집 구하고 있는 사람 누구 알고 있어?

데릭: 음... 친구인 레베카한테 물어볼게. 레베카가 시내에서 더 가까히 살고 싶어 해. 곧 알려줄게!

리즈: 알았어! 정말 고마워. 데릭!

(3 일 후...)

데릭: 안녕, 리즈. 아직도 룸메이트 찾고 있어?

리즈: 응!

데릭: 레베카와 얘기해봤는데 너와 같이 사는 것에 관심 있대. 너와 얘기하고 아파트를 보고 싶어해.

리즈: 좋은 소식이네! 물론이지. 내 전화번호를 레베카에게 줘.

데릭: 응 그럴게. 딱 한 가지 문제가 있어.

리즈: 이런. 뭔데?

데릭: 레베카가 고양이 한 마리를 길러. 근데 너 고양이 싫어하잖아.

리즈: 으.

데릭: 맞아...

리즈: 글쎄... 고양이 착해?

데릭: 응. 그 고양이 정말 멋져. 개냥이야.

리즈: 진짜?

데릭: 응.

리즈: 알았어. 레베카와 고양이를 만나 볼게. 누가 알겠어? 내가 고양이를 좋아하게 될지!

데릭: 하하, 맞아! 마음을 열어봐. 너 룸메이트 진짜 필요하잖아.

리즈. 네 말이 맞아. 그럴게.

NEW ROOMMATE

Liz: Hi, Derek!

Derek: Hey, Liz! How are you?

Liz: I'm good, but I'm a little stressed.

Derek: Why?

Liz: I need to find a new roommate quickly.

Derek: Did Sarah move out?

Liz: Yeah. She got a job in L.A.

Derek: Oh, that's great! For her...

Liz: Yeah, for her! She was the perfect roommate. I don't know how I will find someone as good as her.

Derek: Well, maybe you won't find the perfect roommate, but you can find someone good!

Liz: I hope so. Do you know anyone who needs a place to live?

Derek: Hmm... I'll ask my friend Rebecca. She wants to live closer to the city. I'll let you know soon!

Liz: Okay! Thanks so much, Derek!

(Three days later...)

Derek: Hey, Liz. Are you still trying to find a roommate?

Liz: Yes!

Derek: I talked to Rebecca and she said she is interested in living with you. She wants to talk to you and see the apartment.

Liz: That's great news! Sure. Give her my number.

Derek: I will. There's only one problem.

Liz: Uh oh. What is it?

Derek: She has a cat. I know you hate cats.

Liz: Ugh.

Derek: Yeah...

Liz: Well… is the cat nice?

Derek: Actually, yes. The cat is really cool. It acts like a dog.

Liz: Really?

Derek: Yes.

Liz: Okay. I'll meet Rebecca and the cat. Who knows? Maybe I will start to like cats!

Derek: Ha ha, yes! Keep an open mind. You really need a roommate.

Liz. You're right. I will.

7

여름 피크닉

-

A SUMMER PICNIC (A1)

준: 난 남부 캘리포니아에 사는 것이 너무 좋아. 여기 여름이 정말 멋져!

파올로: 나도 그래. 오늘 날씨가 아름답다.

준: 오늘 밖에서 뭐 좀 하고 싶은데, 나와 같이 할래?

파올로: 물론이지. 뭐 하고 싶어?

준: 피크닉 가고 싶어. 나한테 이미 피크닉 바구니랑 피크닉 담요가 있거든.

파올로: 완벽해. 우리 공원에 가면 될 것 같아.

준: 공원 좋다! 피크닉에서 뭘 먹어야 할까?

파올로: 샌드위치 먹자.

준: 빵은 내가 빵집에서 갓 구운 걸로 사갈 수 있어.

파올로: 나한테 햄과 얇게 썬 칠면조 고기가 있고, 또 상추와 토마토도 있어.

준: 너희 집에 머스터드 소스 있어?

파올로: 아니. 너는?

준: 없어. 내가 머스터드 소스를 사 갈게.

파올로: 마요네즈 좋아해?

준: 응. 마요네즈 있어?

파올로: 응, 있어. 내가 마요네즈 가져갈게.

준: 피크닉에서 뭐 마실래?

파올로: 흠... 물과 탄산음료?

준: 물은 있는데 탄산음료는 없어.

파올로: 우리집에 탄산음료 있어. 물은 네가 가져오면 되고, 탄산음료는 내가 가져갈게.

준: 좋아.

파올로: 공원에서 몇 시에 만날까?

준: 오전 10 시에 만나자.

파올로: 좋아, 거기서 보자!

A SUMMER PICNIC

June: I love living in southern California. The summers here are so nice!

Paolo: I agree. The weather is beautiful today.

June: I want to do something outside today. Would you like to join me?

Paolo: Sure. What do you want to do?

June: I want to have a picnic. I already have a picnic basket and a picnic blanket.

Paolo: Perfect. We can go to the park.

June: The park sounds great! What should we eat at our picnic?

Paolo: We should eat sandwiches.

June: I can buy fresh bread at the bakery.

Paolo: I have ham and sliced turkey. I also have lettuce and tomatoes.

June: Do you have mustard at home?

Paolo: No. Do you?

June: No. I will buy the mustard.

Paolo: Do you like mayonnaise?

June: Yes. Do you have mayonnaise?

Paolo: Yes, I do. I will bring the mayonnaise.

June: What would you like to drink at our picnic?

Paolo: Hmmm... maybe water and soda?

June: I have water but I don't have soda.

Paolo: I have soda at home. You can bring the water and I will bring the soda.

June: That sounds good.

Paolo: What time should we meet at the park?

June: We should meet at 10 a.m.

Paolo: Okay, I'll see you there!

8

어디서 오셨어요?

-

WHERE ARE YOU FROM? (A1)

올리: 안녕하세요. 올리비아예요. 올리라고 불러도 돼요.

프랭크: 안녕하세요, 올리. 프랭크라고 해요. 만나서 반갑습니다.

올리: 저도 만나서 반갑습니다.

프랭크: 어디 출신이신가요?

올리: 영국이요. 올리 씨는요?

프랭크: 저는 미국 알래스카에서 왔어요.

올리: 오, 알래스카요? 알래스카 사진을 본 적이 있어요. 아름다운 곳이에요.

프랭크: 정말 아름다워요. 영국 어디서 오셨어요?

올리: 알프리스톤이라는 작은 도시예요. 런던에서 두 시간 반 정도 떨어진 곳에 있어요.

프랭크: 그렇군요. 알프리스톤은 어떤 곳이에요?

올리: 정말 아기자기하고 오래된 곳이예요. 많은 건물이 천삼백 년대 것이에요.

프랭크: 와.

올리: 네, 마을은 정말로 매력적이에요. 거기에는 영국식 전통 술집들도 있어요.

프랭크: 좋네요. 언젠가 꼭 보고 싶어요!

올리: 꼭 가봐야 해요! 그럼 프랭크 씨는 알래스카 어디에서 왔어요?

프랭크: 알래스카 최대 도시인 앵커리지에서 왔어요.

올리: 거기에 얼마나 많은 사람이 살아요?

프랭크: 삼십만 명쯤 되는 것 같아요.

올리: 와. 좀 작네요.

프랭크: 하하, 네. 알래스카 인구가 그렇게 많지 않아요.

올리: 앵커리지에서 할 수 있는 재미있는 일에는 뭐가 있어요?

프랭크: 알래스카 원주민 센터를 가보실 수 있는데, 알래스카 토착민에 대한 박물관이에요. 거기에는 지진 공원, 글렌 알프스 등산로, 포인트 워론조프와 같이 드라이브하기에 아름다운 곳도 있어요.

올리: 사진 있어요?

프랭크: 네! 보여줄게요.

WHERE ARE YOU FROM?

Ollie: Hi. I'm Olivia, but you can call me Ollie.

Frank: Hey, Ollie. I'm Frank. Nice to meet you.

Ollie: Nice to meet you, too.

Frank: Where are you from?

Ollie: England. What about you?

Frank: I'm from Alaska.

Ollie: Oh, Alaska? I've seen pictures of Alaska. It's beautiful there.

Frank: It's very beautiful. Where in England are you from?

Ollie: A small town called Alfriston. It's about two and a half hours outside of London.

Frank: I see. What is Alfriston like?

Ollie: It's really cute and old. Many of the buildings are from the 1300s.

Frank: Oh, wow.

Ollie: Yeah, the town is really charming. There are some traditional English pubs there, too.

Frank: Sounds great. I would love to see it someday!

Ollie: You should go! So, where in Alaska are you from?

Frank: Anchorage, the biggest city.

Ollie: How many people live there?

Frank: I think almost three hundred thousand.

Ollie: Wow. That's kind of small.

Frank: Ha ha, yeah. Alaska's population isn't very big.

Ollie: What are some fun things to do in Anchorage?

Frank: You can visit the Alaska Native Heritage Center. It is a museum about the indigenous people of Alaska. There are also some beautiful places you can drive to, like Earthquake Park, Glen Alps Trailhead, and Point Woronzof.

Ollie: Do you have pictures of those places?

Frank: Yes! I'll show you.

9

장거리 자동차 여행을 가자

-

LET'S TAKE A ROAD TRIP (A1)

키건: 심심해.

제니: 나도.

키건: 뭘 할 수 있을까?

제니: 몰라.

키건: 흠...

제니: 어딘가로 가고 싶어.

키건: 어디?

제니: 잘 모르겠어. 어디론가 운전해서 가고 싶어.

키건: 좋은 생각이야! 장거리 자동차 여행을 가자!

제니: 좋아. 어디로 가야 할까?

키건: 몰라. 북쪽으로 가야 할 것 같아.

제니: 그래. 해안선을 따라 운전해서 샌프란시스코에 가도 될 것 같은데.

키건: 그거 괜찮다. 가는 길에 몬터레이에 들러도 되겠네.

제니: 응! 나 몬터레이 수족관에 가고 싶어.

키건: 나도. 몬터레이 수족관에서 해달을 보고 싶어.

제니: 해달 너무 귀엽지!

키건: 맞아.

제니: 언제 가고 싶어?

키건: 나는 지금 당장 가고 싶은데, 넌 지금 당장 갈 수 있어??

제니: 응! 장거리 여행 중에 먹을 간식을 좀 사야할 것 같아.

키건: 어떤 간식이 좋아?

제니: 소고기 육포와 감자 칩을 사고 싶어.

키건: 소고기 육포는 장거리 여행에 완벽해!

제니: 맞아.

키건: 나 너무 신나!

제니: 가자!

LET'S TAKE A ROAD TRIP

Keegan: I'm bored.

Jennie: Me too.

Keegan: What can we do?

Jennie: I don't know.

Keegan: Hmm...

Jennie: I want to go somewhere.

Keegan: Where?

Jennie: I'm not sure. I know I want to drive somewhere.

Keegan: Great idea! Let's go on a road trip!

Jennie: That sounds good. Where should we go?

Keegan: I don't know. I think we should drive north.

Jennie: Okay. We can drive along the coast and visit San Francisco.

Keegan: I like that idea. We can also stop at Monterey!

Jennie: Yes! I want to go to the Monterey Aquarium.

Keegan: Me too. I want to see the sea otters at the Monterey Aquarium.

Jennie: Sea otters are so cute!

Keegan: I agree.

Jennie: When do you want to go?

Keegan: I want to go right now. Can you go right now?

Jennie: Yep! We need snacks for the road trip though.

Keegan: Which snacks would you like?

Jennie: I want to get beef jerky and potato chips.

Keegan: Beef jerky is perfect for road trips!

Jennie: I agree.

Keegan: I'm so excited!

Jennie: Let's go!

10

뒷마당 바비큐 파티

-

BACKYARD BBQ (A1)

질: 안녕하세요, 윌슨 씨. 잘 지내세요?

윌슨: 안녕하세요, 질 씨! 전 잘 지내요. 잘 지내세요?

질: 잘 지내죠! 이번 주말에 계획 있어요?

윌슨: 아니요. 이번 주말에 집에 있으려고요. 질 씨는요?

질: 팀이 뒷마당에서 바비큐를 하고 싶어 해요. 저희 바비큐 파티에 오시겠어요?

윌슨: 가고 싶어요! 언제인가요?

질: 토요일 정오예요.

윌슨: 좋아요! 바비큐 파티에서 어떤 음식을 먹을 건가요?

질: 핫도그, 햄버거, 바비큐 치킨을 먹을 거예요.

윌슨: 맛있겠네요!

질: 그러길 바래요.

윌슨: 제가 가져갈 것이 있나요?

질: 네, 모두 먹을 수 있는 샐러드나 디저트를 가져오시면 될 것 같아요.

윌슨: 그렇게 할게요. 바비큐 파티에 몇 명이 오나요?

질: 열다섯 명 정도 될 것 같아요.

윌슨: 사람이 많네요!

질: 네, 저희 친구들을 많이 초대했어요.

윌슨: 제 친구를 데려가도 될까요?

질: 물론이죠, 누구예요?

윌슨: 이름은 메리이고, 슈퍼마켓에서 만났어요.

질: 와! 그분을 좋아하나요?

윌슨: 네, 좋아해요. 질 씨가 메리를 만났으면 좋겠어요.

질: 좋아요. 제가 신나네요!

윌슨: 고마워요.

질: 천만에요! 이제 집에 가야 해요. 이번 주 토요일에 봐요.

윌슨: 네, 토요일에 봐요! 기대돼요.

질: 저도요. 안녕히 가세요!

윌슨: 곧 봐요.

BACKYARD BBQ

Jill: Hi, Wilson. How are you doing?

Wilson: Hi there, neighbor! I'm doing well. How are you?

Jill: Fine, thanks! Do you have plans this weekend?

Wilson: No. I'm staying home this weekend. What about you?

Jill: Tim wants to have a barbecue in our backyard. Would you like to come to our barbecue?

Wilson: I would love to! When is it?

Jill: Saturday at noon.

Wilson: Great! Which foods will you have at the barbecue?

Jill: We will have hot dogs, hamburgers, and barbecued chicken.

Wilson: That sounds delicious!

Jill: I hope so.

Wilson: Should I bring anything?

Jill: Yes, you can bring a salad or dessert for everyone.

Wilson: I'll do that. How many people are coming to the barbecue?

Jill: I think about fifteen.

Wilson: That is a lot of people!

Jill: Yes, we invited many of our friends.

Wilson: May I bring a friend?

Jill: Sure, who is it?

Wilson: Her name is Mary. I met her at the supermarket.

Jill: Oh, wow! Do you like her?

Wilson: Yes, I do. I want you to meet her.

Jill: That sounds good. I'm excited for you!

Wilson: Thank you.

Jill: You're welcome! I have to go home now, but I will see you this Saturday.

Wilson: Yes, see you this Saturday! I'm looking forward to it.

Jill: Me too. Goodbye!

Wilson: See you later.

11

두 번째 첫 데이트

-

A SECOND FIRST DATE (A1)

다리우스: 안녕하세요. 카산드라 씨인가요?

카산드라: 네! 다리우스 씨인가요?

다리우스: 네, 만나서 반갑습니다!

카산드라: 저도 만나서 반갑습니다. 오늘 하루 어땠어요?

다리우스: 좀 바빴어요. 오늘 하루 어땠어요?

카산드라: 저도 바빴어요.

다리우스: 음, 배가 출출하시죠?

카산드라: 네, 배가 고파서 뭐 좀 먹어야 될 것 같아요.

다리우스: 좋아요! 무엇을 드시겠어요?

카산드라: 생선이 맛있을 것 같네요.

다리우스: 저도 생선이 맛있을 것 같아요. 제가 생선을 주문할게요.

카산드라: 좋아요!

다리우스: 카산드라씨 얘기 좀 해 주세요. 무슨 일을 하세요?

카산드라: 저는 법률 사무소에서 일해요. 변호사거든요.

다리우스: 오, 멋지네요. 일은 마음에 들어요?

카산드라: 많이 어렵지만 변호사인 것이 좋아요.

다리우스: 회사의 어떤 점이 좋으세요?

카산드라: 우리 회사 모두가 매우 친절해요. 그리고 스무 가지의 커피를 만드는 커피 머신도 있어요.

다리우스: 와! 잠깐... 커피 머신이 하얀색인가요?

카산드라: 네, 어떻게 아셨어요?

다리우스: 카산드라 씨 상사께서 모두를 위해 커피 머신을 샀나요?

카산드라: 네... 잠깐. 혹시 은행에서 일하시나요?

다리우스: 네...

카산드라: 우리가 전에 데이트했었나요?

다리우스: 네... 그런 것 같아요. 이거 민망하네요. 음, 다시 만나서 반갑습니다!

카산드라: 아, 저도 다시 만나서 반갑습니다!

A SECOND FIRST DATE

Darius: Hey. Are you Cassandra?

Cassandra: Yes! Are you Darius?

Darius: Yes, nice to meet you!

Cassandra: Nice to meet you, too. How was your day?

Darius: Pretty busy. How was your day?

Cassandra: Mine was busy, too.

Darius: Well, I hope you're hungry.

Cassandra: I'm hungry and ready to eat.

Darius: Great! What would you like to eat?

Cassandra: I think the fish looks good.

Darius: I think the fish looks good, too. I'll order the fish for us.

Cassandra: Okay!

Darius: So tell me about yourself. What do you do for work?

Cassandra: I work at a law firm. I'm a lawyer.

Darius: Oh, cool. Do you like your job?

Cassandra: It's very hard, but I love being a lawyer. I also love my firm.

Darius: What do you love about your firm?

Cassandra: Everyone is very nice at my firm. Also, we have a coffee machine that makes twenty different kinds of coffee drinks.

Darius: Wow! Wait... is this coffee machine white?

Cassandra: Yes, how did you know?

Darius: Did your boss buy the coffee machine for everyone?

Cassandra: Yes... wait. Do you work at a bank?

Darius: Yes...

Cassandra: Did we go on a date before?

Darius: Yes... I think we did. This is awkward. Well, nice to meet you again!

Cassandra: Uh, nice to meet you again, too!

12

누구와 같이 살아?

-

WHO DO YOU LIVE WITH? (A1)

로렌조: 안녕, 엘레나. 피곤해?

엘레나: 응, 조금. 어젯밤에 잠을 잘 못 잤어.

로렌조: 진짜? 왜?

엘레나: 언니네 아기가 밤새 울었어.

로렌조: 이런. 정말 불편했겠다.

엘레나: 맞아 불편했어.

로렌조: 아기는 몇 살이야?

엘레나: 삼 개월이야.

로렌조: 와, 엄청 어리네! 맞아, 그 나이 때 아기들은 많이 울어.

엘레나: 응. 나 혼자 살고 싶은데 이 도시의 아파트가 너무 비싸.

로렌조: 응, 맞아.

엘레나: 너는 누구랑 같이 살아?

로렌조: 친구 마테오랑. 우리는 방 두 개 짜리 아파트에 살고 있어.

엘레나: 좋다. 그는 좋은 룸메이트야?

로렌조: 응, 그는 정말로 좋은 룸메이트야. 그런데 코를 크게 골아!

엘레나: 아, 그래?

로렌조: 응. 나는 매일 밤 귀마개를 하고 자. 가끔 잠을 설치기도 해.

엘레나: 그럼 우리는 비슷한 문제가 있네! 내 룸메이트가 아기인 것만 빼면.

로렌조: 하하, 맞아! 몇 달 후에는 네 룸메이트가 그렇게 많이 울지 않아야 할텐데. 마테오가 코 고는 걸 멈출지는 모르겠네!

엘레나: 나도 그렇게 되기를 바래! 그래도 나는 내 조카를 사랑해.

너무 귀여워.

로렌조: 너는 네 조카와 많은 시간을 함께 보낼 수 있으니 복 받은 거야.

엘레나: 알고 있지.

로렌조: 좋아, 난 가야 해. 오늘 밤에 잘 수 있길 바래!

엘레나: 나도 그러길 바래!

WHO DO YOU LIVE WITH?

Lorenzo: Hey, Elena. Are you tired?

Elena: Yeah, a little. I didn't sleep much last night.

Lorenzo: Really? Why not?

Elena: My sister's baby was crying all night.

Lorenzo: Oh, no. That's not fun for anyone.

Elena: No, it's not.

Lorenzo: How old is the baby?

Elena: He's three months.

Lorenzo: Oh, he's super young! Yeah, babies cry a lot at that age.

Elena: Yep. I want to live alone but apartments in this city are so expensive.

Lorenzo: Yes, they are.

Elena: Who do you live with?

Lorenzo: My friend Matteo. We have a two-bedroom apartment.

Elena: Cool. Is he a good roommate?

Lorenzo: Yeah, he's a really good roommate. But he snores loudly!

Elena: Oh, he does?

Lorenzo: Yeah. I wear ear plugs almost every night. Sometimes I don't sleep very well.

Elena: So we have a similar problem! Except my roommate is a baby.

Lorenzo: Ha ha, true! And hopefully in a few months your roommate will stop crying so much. I don't know if Matteo will stop snoring!

Elena: I hope so! I love my nephew, though. He's so cute.

Lorenzo: You're lucky that you can spend so much time with him.

Elena: I know.

Lorenzo: Okay, well, I have to go. I hope you can sleep tonight!

Elena: Me too!

13

내가 좋아하는 선생님

-

MY FAVORITE TEACHER (A1)

캐리: 안녕, 라제시. 잘 지내?

라제시: 안녕, 캐리. 응 잘 지내. 뭐 하고 있어?

캐리: 고등학교 때 찍은 사진을 보고 있어.

라제시: 와, 멋지다. 나도 좀 볼 수 있을까?

캐리: 물론.

라제시: 이 여자 애들은 누구야?

캐리: 내 친구 엘레나와 레이첼이야. 고등학교 때 가장 친한 친구들이었어.

라제시: 좋네! 아직도 얘네들이랑 친구야?

캐리: 응. 엘레나는 포틀랜드에 살아서 항상 보고, 레이첼은 지난 주에 봤어. 레이첼은 뉴욕에 사는데, 가족들 보러 포틀랜드에 왔더라고. 우리 모두 같이 저녁을 먹었어. 레이첼은 일 년에 한두 번밖에 보지 못하니까 반갑더라.

라제시: 멋지네. 내 고등학교 친구 대부분은 다른 도시에 살고 있어서 자주 못 봐.

캐리: 이런, 안타깝네.

라제시: 응, 그래도 우리 계속 연락하고 있으니까 괜찮아.

캐리: 잘됐네.

라제시: 저 사람은 누구야?

캐리: 번 선생님이셔. 내 사진 선생님이셨어.

라제시: 오, 사진을 찍었었어?

캐리: 응! 고등학교 때 내가 사진을 좋아했어. 사실 나 대학에서

미술을 공부했었거든.

라제시: 그랬어?

캐리: 응, 그런데 이 년 후에 전공을 바꿨어. 사진 찍는 걸 직업말고 취미로 하기로 결정했어.

라제시: 그건 아마도 좋은 생각이었을 거야. 번 선생님과 아직도 연락해?

캐리: 사실, 그래! 내가 좋아하는 선생님이셔! 내가 선생님 덕분에 사진 찍는 걸 좋아해.

라제시: 정말 멋있다! 나는 내가 좋아하는 선생님과 연락하지는 않지만, 나는 그 선생님께 정말 감사해.

캐리: 선생님들께서는 대단하셔.

라제시: 맞아, 대단하셔.

MY FAVORITE TEACHER

Carrie: Hey, Rajesh. How are you?

Rajesh: Hi, Carrie. I'm pretty good. What are you up to?

Carrie: I'm looking at pictures from high school.

Rajesh: Oh, cool. Can I see some?

Carrie: Sure.

Rajesh: Who are those girls?

Carrie: Those are my friends, Alana and Rachel. They were my best friends in high school.

Rajesh: Nice! Are you still friends with them?

Carrie: Yeah. Alana lives in Portland, so I see her all the time. And I saw Rachel last week. She lives in New York but she came back to Portland to visit her family, and we all had dinner. I only see her once or twice a year, so it was nice to see her.

Rajesh: That's awesome. Most of my friends from high school live in different cities so I don't see them very often.

Carrie: Aw, that's too bad.

Rajesh: Yeah, but we keep in touch, so it's okay.

Carrie: Good.

Rajesh: Who's that guy?

Carrie: That's Mr. Byrne. He was my photography teacher.

Rajesh: Oh, you took photography?

Carrie: Yep! I loved photography in high school. I actually studied art in college.

Rajesh: You did?

Carrie: Yeah, but I changed majors after two years. I decided I only wanted to do photography for fun, not as a job.

Rajesh: That was probably a good idea. Do you still talk to Mr. Byrne?

Carrie: Actually, yes! He was my favorite teacher! I love photography because of him.

Rajesh: That's so cool! I didn't keep in touch with my favorite teacher, but I am very grateful for her.

Carrie: Teachers are amazing.

Rajesh: Yes, they are!

14

해변에서 산책

-

A WALK ON THE BEACH (A1)

린: 정말 아름다운 날이야!

아다무: 응, 맞아. 해변에서 산책하기에 완벽한 날이야!

린: 해변 가까이 살다니 우리 정말 운이 좋다.

아다무: 맞아. 우리 해변에 더 자주 오자.

린: 맞아. 그러자. 발 밑에 있는 모래 느낌이 참 좋다.

아다무: 맞아. 그런데 가끔 모래가 뜨거워!

린: 그러네. 그래도 지금은 기분이 좋아.

아다무: 응.

린: 나는 조개껍데기를 좀 모을거야.

아다무: 재미있겠다. 나는 수영을 좀 하려고 해. 바다가 나를 부르는 것 같아.

린: 알았어! 조심해!

아다무: 너무 멀리는 가지 않을 거야. 몇 분 정도만 수영하고 싶어. 그리고 나는 수영을 잘해.

린: 알았어.

(십분 뒤...)

아다무: 너무 시원해! 좋은 조개껍데기 좀 찾았어?

린: 응, 조금. 이것 봐.

아다무: 와, 멋지다! 색이 화려하네.

린: 물이 차가웠어?

아다무: 처음에는 차가웠는데 나중에는 괜찮았어. 그런데 파도는 조금 강했어.

린: 응, 파도가 강해 보였어!

아다무: 나 잠깐 모래 위에 앉아서 몸을 말릴게.

린: 알았어. 나는 조개껍데기를 더 많이 찾아볼게. 곧 돌아올게!

아다무: 재미있게 놀아!

A WALK ON THE BEACH

Lynn: It's such a beautiful day!

Adamu: Yes, it is. A perfect day for a walk on the beach!

Lynn: We're so lucky that we live close to the beach.

Adamu: Yeah. We should come more often.

Lynn: Yes, we should. I love the feeling of the sand under my feet.

Adamu: Me too. But sometimes the sand is hot!

Lynn: True. It feels nice right now, though.

Adamu: Yeah.

Lynn: I think I will collect some shells.

Adamu: That sounds fun. I think I will go for a swim. The water looks so inviting.

Lynn: Okay! Be careful!

Adamu: I won't go out very far. I just want to swim for a couple minutes. And I'm a good swimmer.

Lynn: All right.

(Ten minutes later...)

Adamu: That was so refreshing! Did you find some good shells?

Lynn: Yes, a few. Look at this one.

Adamu: Oh, that's cool! It's so colorful.

Lynn: Was the water cold?

Adamu: It was cold at first, but then it felt good. The waves were a little strong, though.

Lynn: Yeah, they looked strong!

Adamu: I will sit on the sand for a while so I can dry off.

Lynn: Okay. I will look for some more shells. I will be back soon!

Adamu: Have fun!

15

언어를 배우는 가장 좋은 방법

-

BEST WAYS TO LEARN A LANGUAGE (A1)

미첼: 일본어 실력을 향상시키고 싶어.

레이시: 일본어를 할 줄 알아?

미첼: 응, 조금.

레이시: 그건 몰랐네.

미첼: 삼사년 전부터 일본어를 배우기 시작했어.

레이시: 진짜? 왜?

미첼: 그 언어와 문화가 좋아. 내가 어렸을 때 일본에 갔었는데, 그 후로 항상 일본에 관심이 있었어.

레이시: 흥미롭다. 일본어 공부는 어떻게 했어?

미첼: 온라인 강좌를 듣기도 하고, 휴대폰에 앱도 있어. 하지만 정말 실력이 늘지 않아.

레이시: 일본 영화나 텔레비전 프로를 봐?

미첼: 가끔.

레이시: 아마 그런 걸 더 자주 봐야 할 거야.

미첼: 노력하고 있어. 그런데 가끔 대화를 이해하기 어려울 때가 있어.

레이시: 일본어 자막과 함께 보려고 해봐. 그러면 일본어를 읽으면서 동시에 들을 수도 있어. 그러면 듣기와 말하기 실력에 도움이 될 거야.

미첼: 그건 좋은 생각이야. 또 어떤 것들을 해야 할까?

레이시: 일본 사람들이랑 대화해 본 적 있어?

미첼: 그런 적 없어.

레이시: 내 친구는 일본어와 영어 언어 문화 교환 그룹을 하더라고. 너도 그 그룹에 가입하면 좋을 것 같아. 한 달에 한 번 만나서 영어와 일본어를 연습하더라고.

미첼: 와, 너무 좋은데!

레이시: 내가 정보를 알아봐 줄게!

BEST WAYS TO LEARN A LANGUAGE

Mitchell: I want to improve my Japanese.

Lacey: You speak Japanese?

Mitchell: Yes, a little.

Lacey: I didn't know that.

Mitchell: I started learning Japanese three or four years ago.

Lacey: Really? Why?

Mitchell: I love the language and the culture. I went to Japan when I was a child. After that, I have always been interested in Japan.

Lacey: That's interesting. How do you study Japanese?

Mitchell: I take an online course and I have an app on my phone. But I'm not really getting better.

Lacey: Do you watch Japanese movies or TV shows?

Mitchell: Sometimes.

Lacey: Maybe you should watch them more often.

Mitchell: I try to. But sometimes it's hard to understand the dialogue.

Lacey: Try watching with Japanese subtitles. Then you can read Japanese and listen at the same time. Doing that will help both your listening and your speaking skills.

Mitchell: That's a good idea. What else should I do?

Lacey: Do you ever speak to Japanese people?

Mitchell: Not really.

Lacey: My friend is in a Japanese and English language and cultural exchange group. You should join the group. They meet once a month and practice English and Japanese.

Mitchell: Oh, that sounds perfect!

Lacey: I will get the information for you!

16

저게 무슨 소리야?

-

WHAT'S THAT SOUND? (A1)

클레어: 저게 무슨 소리야?

에르네스토: 무슨 소리?

클레어: 저거 안 들려?

에르네스토: 응...

클레어: 개구리 소리 같아.

에르네스토: 개구리?

클레어: 응.

에르네스토: 아무 소리도 안 들려.

클레어: 소리가 큰데!

에르네스토: 네가 그 소리를 상상하고 있을 지도 모르지.

클레어: 아니야. 네가 귀가 안 들리는 걸지도 몰라!

에르네스토: 귀 엄청 잘 들려.

클레어: 저기! 나 또 들었어.

에르네스토: 흠... 나도 들었어. 네가 맞아. 개구리 소리 같아.

클레어: 아하! 내가 말했잖아!

에르네스토: 그런데 우리는 도시에 살아. 여기에 개구리는 안살아.

클레어: 누군가의 애완동물이었는데 집에서 탈출을 했을지도 몰라.

에르네스토: 찾아보자.

클레어: 알았어!

에르네스토: 너는 건물 뒤쪽을 찾아봐. 나는 건물 앞쪽을 찾아볼게.

클레어: 건물 뒤쪽은 무서워. 내가 건물 앞쪽을 찾아볼게.

에르네스토: 좋아. 휴대폰 손전등을 사용해.

클레어: 좋은 생각이야.

에르네스토: 찾았다!

클레어: 찾았어?!

에르네스토: 오, 잠깐, 아니야. 그냥 돌이었네.

클레어: 찾은 것 같아!

에르네스토: 오 이런! 보여!

클레어:너무 귀엽다! 우리가 그냥 데리고 갈까?

에르네스토: 안돼, 귀여워도 야생동물을 데리고 갈 순 없어.

클레어: 으, 알았어. 어쨌든, 재미있는 자연 산책이었어!

에르네스토: 하하, 맞아 그랬어!

WHAT'S THAT SOUND?

Claire: What's that sound?

Ernesto: What sound?

Claire: You don't hear that?

Ernesto: No...

Claire: It sounds like a frog.

Ernesto: A frog?

Claire: Yeah.

Ernesto: I don't hear anything.

Claire: But it's loud!

Ernesto: Maybe you're imagining the sound.

Claire: No, maybe you just have bad hearing!

Ernesto: My hearing is amazing.

Claire: There! I heard it again.

Ernesto: Hmm... I heard that. You're right. It sounds like a frog.

Claire: Aha! I told you!

Ernesto: But we live in the city. There are no frogs here.

Claire: Maybe it was someone's pet and it escaped from their house.

Ernesto: Let's look for it.

Claire: Okay!

Ernesto: You look behind the building. I'll look in front of the building.

Claire: It's scary behind the building. I'll look in front.

Ernesto: Fine. Use the flashlight on your phone.

Claire: Good idea.

Ernesto: I found it!

Claire: You did?!

Ernesto: Oh, wait, no. That's just a rock.

Claire: I think I found it!

Ernesto: Oh my gosh! I see it!

Claire: He's so cute! Can we keep him?

Ernesto: No, we can't keep wild animals, even if they are cute.

Claire: Ugh, fine. Well, this was a fun nature walk!

Ernesto: Ha ha, yes it was!

17

달리기는 힘들어

-

RUNNING IS HARD (A1)

카일리: 마르쿠스, 나랑 같이 달리기 할래?

마르쿠스: 음... 별로.

카일리: 왜?

마르쿠스: 난 뛰는 거 안 좋아해.

카일리: 안 좋아해? 근데 너 건강하잖아.

마르쿠스: 응, 나는 헬스장에 가서 아령를 들어. 그리고 가끔 농구도 해. 근데 장거리 달리기는 별로야.

카일리: 나랑 같이 뛰면 천천히 뛰어도 되고 휴식도 많이 취해도 돼.

마르쿠스: 흠... 알았어. 갈게.

카일리: 앗싸!

마르쿠스: 언제 갈 거야?

카일리: 지금.

마르쿠스: 아, 진짜? 알았어. 운동화 신고 올게.

카일리: 알았어.

마르쿠스: 준비!

카일리: 가자!

마르쿠스: 야, 천천히 가자!

카일리: 난 천천히 가고 있어!

마르쿠스: 더 천천히 가면 안돼?

카일리: 이것보다 더 천천히 가면, 걷는 거나 마찬가지야.

마르쿠스: 윽, 달리기는 힘들어!

카일리: 처음에는 힘들어. 그런데 점점 더 쉬워져. 일주일에 두세 번씩 단거리라도 달리도록 노력 해야 해. 그러면 더 쉬워질 거야.

마르쿠스: 알았어, 그렇게 해볼게.

카일리: 그리고 너는 내가 아령 드는 걸 도와주면 되고. 우린 서로 도울 수 있어.

마르쿠스: 좋아!

RUNNING IS HARD

Kylie: Do you want to go running with me, Marcus?

Marcus: Umm... not really.

Kylie: Why not?

Marcus: I don't like running.

Kylie: You don't? But you're in good shape.

Marcus: Yeah, I go to the gym and lift weights. And I play basketball sometimes. But I don't like running long distances.

Kylie: If you go with me, we can run slowly and take lots of breaks.

Marcus: Hmm... okay. I'll go.

Kylie: Yay!

Marcus: When are you going?

Kylie: Now.

Marcus: Ah, really? Okay. Let me put my running shoes on.

Kylie: All right.

Marcus: Ready!

Kylie: Let's go!

Marcus: Hey, slow down!

Kylie: I am going slowly!

Marcus: Can you go more slowly?

Kylie: If we go more slowly, we will be walking.

Marcus: Ugh, running is hard!

Kylie: It's hard in the beginning. But it gets easier. You should try to run two or three times a week, just short distances. And then it will get easier.

Marcus: Okay, I'll try that.

Kylie: And you can help me lift weights. We can help each other.

Marcus: Deal!

18

쿠키 굽기

-

BAKING COOKIES (A1)

베티: 우리 한동안 쿠키를 안 구웠네.
덩컨: 네 말이 맞아. 나 지금 쿠키가 먹고 싶어.
베티: 나도.
덩컨: 좀 구워 먹을까?
베티: 좋아!
덩컨: 어떤 쿠키를 굽지?
베티: 두 가지 다른 종류로 구울 수 있어?
덩컨: 물론! 어떤 거?
베티: 나는 초콜릿 칩 쿠키랑 스니커두들을 원해.
덩컨: 아주 좋아. 우리 밀가루나 설탕 있어?
베티: 아니, 없어. 냉동실에 얼린 쿠키 반죽은 있어.
덩컨: 완벽해! 그게 굽기가 쉬워.
베티: 여기 있어. 빵 굽는 팬 있어?
덩컨: 응, 여기 있어.
베티: 좋아! 이제, 오븐 좀 켜줄래?
덩컨: 응.
베티: 화씨 350 도까지 오븐을 데워 줄래?
덩컨: 알았어. 쿠키 반죽을 도와줄까?
베티: 좋아! 칼로 반죽을 작은 조각으로 잘라줘.
덩컨: 알았어. 이제 어떻게 해?
베티: 그 작은 조각으로 공을 만들어. 그러고 나서 빵 굽는 팬에 올려줘.

덩컨: 알았어. 쿠키 반죽 먹어도 돼?

베티: 아니.

덩컨: 하지만 쿠키 반죽은 너무 맛있는 걸!

베티: 너한테 좋지 않아!

BAKING COOKIES

Betty: We haven't baked cookies in a long time.

Duncan: You're right. I want cookies now.

Betty: Me too.

Duncan: Do you want to bake some?

Betty: Sure!

Duncan: What kind of cookies should we bake?

Betty: Can we bake two different kinds?

Duncan: Sure! Which kinds?

Betty: I want chocolate chip cookies and snickerdoodles.

Duncan: Awesome. Do we have any flour or sugar?

Betty: No, we don't. I have frozen cookie dough in the freezer.

Duncan: Perfect! Those are easy to bake.

Betty: Here you go. Do you have a baking pan?

Duncan: Yes, I do. Here it is.

Betty: Great! Now, can you turn on the oven?

Duncan: Yes.

Betty: Can you heat the oven to three hundred fifty degrees Fahrenheit?

Duncan: Okay. Do you want help with the cookie dough?

Betty: Sure! Cut a small piece with a knife.

Duncan: Got it. What now?

Betty: Make a ball with that small piece. Then, put the ball on the baking pan.

Duncan: Okay. Can we eat the cookie dough?

Betty: No.

Duncan: But the cookie dough is so delicious!

Betty: It's not good for you!

19

고래 관광

-

WHALE WATCHING (A1)

자니나: 오늘 고래 관광하러 가는 거 너무 신나!

크리산토: 나도 그래.

자니나: 몇 년 전에 고래 관광하러 갔을 때 기억나? 우리 대여섯 마리 봤잖아!

크리산토: 정말 멋졌어. 아마 오늘도 운이 좋아서 고래를 많이 볼 수 있을 거야!

자니나: 그러길 바래.

크리산토: 재킷 가져왔어? 조금 추울 거야.

자니나: 응, 그리고 스카프랑 장갑도 가져왔어.

크리산토: 좋아. 아, 배가 움직인다! 자, 간다!

자니나: 야호! 나 돌고래도 봤으면 좋겠어. 우리 지난번에 돌고래 많이 봤잖아!

크리산토: 알아. 돌고래 너무 좋아.

자니나: 나도. 내가 가장 좋아하는 동물이 돌고래인 것 같아.

크리산토: 고래보다 더?

자니나: 응.

크리산토: 쉿. 너무 크게 말하지 마. 고래들이 슬플 거야.

자니나: 이런, 알았어.

(삼십 분 후…)

크리산토: 봐!

자니나: 어디?

크리산토: 저기!

자니나: 아무것도 안 보여!

크리산토: 저기 있어.

자니나: 보여! 정말 멋지다!

크리산토: 고래 두 마리가 함께 있어! 그리고 고래들이 우리에게 손을 흔들고 있는 것 같아!

자니나: 하하. 안녕, 고래들!

크리산토: 우리 매년 고래 관광을 와야 해!

자니나: 맞아!

WHALE WATCHING

Janina: I'm so excited to go whale watching today!

Crisanto: I am, too.

Janina: Do you remember when we went whale watching a few years ago? We saw five or six whales!

Crisanto: That was so cool. Maybe we will be lucky again and see lots of whales today!

Janina: I hope so.

Crisanto: Did you bring your jacket? It will be a little cold.

Janina: Yes, and I brought a scarf and gloves, too.

Crisanto: Good. Oh, the boat is moving! Here we go!

Janina: Yay! I also hope we see dolphins. We saw so many dolphins last time!

Crisanto: I know. I love dolphins.

Janina: Me too. I think they are my favorite animal.

Crisanto: More than whales?

Janina: Yeah.

Crisanto: Shh. Don't say that so loud. The whales will be sad.

Janina: Oops, okay.

(30 minutes later...)

Crisanto: Look!

Janina: Where?

Crisanto: Over there!

Janina: I don't see anything!

Crisanto: It's there.

Janina: I see it! So cool!

Crisanto: There are two whales together! And it looks like they're waving to us!

Janina: Ha ha. Hi, whales!

Crisanto: We should go whale watching every year!

Janina: I agree!

20

장거리 비행

-

A LONG FLIGHT (A1)

조안나: 윽, 저는 이번 비행이 신나지 않아요.

프레드: 왜요?

조안나: 10 시간이나 걸리니까요!

프레드: 그렇죠. 하지만 그냥 자면 되잖아요.

조안나: 전 비행기에서 잠을 못 자요.

프레드: 진짜요?

조안나: 네. 프레드 씨는요?

프레드: 네, 저는푹 잘 수 있어요.

조안나: 저는 그렇게 못해요. 너무 불편해요.

프레드: 장거리 비행에서 어떤 걸 하세요?

조안나: 책 읽고 영화 봐요.

프레드: 지루한가요?

조안나: 네, 당연하죠. 그런데 요즘은 비행기에 꽤 괜찮은 영화를 보여줘요. 작년에 비행기에서 영화 네 편을 봤어요.

프레드: 와. 정말 많은 영화를 보셨네요! 어떤 종류의 영화를 보셨나요?

조안나: 액션 영화 한 편, 드라마 두 편, 슬픈 영화 한 편이요. 저는 눈물이 많아서 비행기에서 슬픈 영화를 보지 않으려고 해요!

프레드: 하하, 진짜요?

조안나: 네. 창피해요.

프레드: 글쎄요, 전 비행기에서 잘 때 가끔 코를 고는데요! 우는 것보다 그게 더 창피한 것 같아요.

조안나: 맞네요. 프레드 씨가 이긴 것 같아요! 기분이 나아졌어요.

프레드: 하하. 제가 도움이 되었다니 기쁘네요!

A LONG FLIGHT

Joanna: Ugh, I'm not excited about this flight.

Fred: Why not?

Joanna: Because it's ten hours long!

Fred: Yeah. But you can just sleep.

Joanna: I can't sleep on planes.

Fred: Really?

Joanna: No. Can you?

Fred: Yeah, I can sleep pretty well.

Joanna: I can't. I'm too uncomfortable.

Fred: What do you do on long flights?

Joanna: I read books and watch movies.

Fred: Do you get bored?

Joanna: Yeah, of course. But planes have pretty good movies these days. I watched four movies on my flight last year.

Fred: Wow. That's a lot of movies! What kind of movies did you watch?

Joanna: An action movie, two dramas, and one sad movie. I try not to watch sad movies on planes because I cry a lot!

Fred: Ha ha, really?

Joanna: Yeah. It's embarrassing.

Fred: Well, sometimes I snore when I sleep on planes! I think that's more embarrassing than crying.

Joanna: Yes, I think you win! I feel better now.

Fred: Ha ha. I'm glad I helped!

21

시험 보기

-

TAKING TESTS (A1)

가브리엘: 안녕, 루카. 뭐하고 있어?

루카: 안녕, 가브리엘. 공부하고 있어. 너는?

가브리엘: 나는 지금 수업 사이에 쉬는 시간이어서 앉아서 음악 들을 거야.

루카: 좋네. 나도 쉬고 싶은데 공부해야 돼.

가브리엘: 무슨 공부하고 있어?

루카: 중국 역사.

가브리엘: 아, 어렵겠다.

루카: 맞아. 멋진데 조금 어려워. 기억해야 할 장소와 이름이 너무 많아!

가브리엘: 어떤 종류의 시험이야?

루카: 객관식, 단답식, 그리고 논술식.

가브리엘: 쉬워 보이지 않는데!

루카: 응... 교수님은 좋으신데, 수업이 엄격해. 그래도 많이 배우고 있어.

가브리엘: 멋지네. 얼마 동안 시험을 봐?

루카: 한 시간 반.

가브리엘: 시험 보는 동안 노트를 참고해도 돼?

루카: 아니. 전부 외워야 해.

가브리엘: 그렇구나.

루카: 너는 시험에서 항상 점수를 잘 받잖아. 어떻게 하는 거야?

가브리엘: 하하, 항상 그런 건 아니야! 몰라. 공부를 많이 하는 것 같아.

루카: 나도 공부를 많이 하는데 가끔은 성적이 별로야. 나는 시험을 잘 못 봐.

가브리엘: 네가 원한다면 몇 가지 공부 팁을 줄 수 있어. 아마 너에게 도움이 될 거야.

루카: 좋아!

TAKING TESTS

Gabrielle: Hey, Luca. What are you doing?

Luca: Hi, Gabrielle. I'm studying. What about you?

Gabrielle: I have a break between classes now, so I will sit and listen to some music.

Luca: Cool. I want to relax too, but I have to study.

Gabrielle: What are you studying?

Luca: Chinese history.

Gabrielle: Oh, that sounds hard.

Luca: Yeah. It's cool, but it's a little difficult. There are so many places and names to remember!

Gabrielle: What kind of test is it?

Luca: Multiple choice, short answer, and writing.

Gabrielle: That doesn't sound easy!

Luca: No… the professor is good but her class is tough. I'm learning a lot though.

Gabrielle: That's cool. How long is the test?

Luca: An hour and a half.

Gabrielle: Can you look at your notes during the test?

Luca: No. We have to memorize everything.

Gabrielle: I see.

Luca: You always get good grades on tests. How do you do it?

Gabrielle: Ha ha, not always! I don't know. I guess I study a lot.

Luca: I study a lot, too, but I get bad grades sometimes. I'm not good at tests.

Gabrielle: I can give you some study tips if you want. Maybe they will help you.

Luca: I would love that!

22

헬스장에 가자

-

LET'S GO TO THE GYM (A1)

론: 안녕, 레슬리. 너 지금 바빠?

레슬리: 안녕, 론. 아니, 안 바빠. 무슨 일이야?

론: 헬스장에 가고 싶어. 나랑 같이 갈래?

레슬리: 모르겠어. 나 헬스장 회원권이 없는데.

론: 나도 없어. 헬스장에 가입하려고 생각 중이야.

레슬리: 알았어.

론: 같이 가입하자!

레슬리: 좋아! 어떤 헬스장에 가입하고 싶어?

론: 잘 모르겠어. 운동하고 싶은데 좀 재미있는 걸 하고 싶어.

레슬리: 암벽 등반 좋아해?

론: 모르겠어. 암벽 등반을 해본 적이 없어.

레슬리: 새로운 암벽 등반 헬스장이 저번 주에 문을 열었어.

론: 멋진데! 암벽 등반을 잘해야만 가입할 수 있을까?

레슬리: 아니, 그러지 않아도 돼. 누구라도 가입할 수 있어.

론: 회원권은 얼마야?

레슬리: 회원권은 한 달에 삼십 달러 정도 되는 것 같아. 게다가, 첫 주는 무료야!

론: 대박이네! 네가 암벽 등반을 좋아하는지 몰랐어.

레슬리: 좋아해! 우리 암벽 등반 헬스장에 가입할까?

론: 좋아! 암벽 등반용 신발이 필요해?

레슬리: 아니, 운동화 신어도 돼.

론: 특별한 옷이 필요해?

레슬리: 아니 안 필요해. 평범한 운동복 입어도 돼.

론: 알았어. 신난다!

레슬리: 맞아! 준비 됐어?

론: 응, 해보자!

LET'S GO TO THE GYM

Ron: Hi, Leslie. Are you busy right now?

Leslie: Hi, Ron. No, I'm not. What's up?

Ron: I want to go to the gym. Will you come with me?

Leslie: I don't know. I don't have a gym membership.

Ron: I don't either. I'm thinking of joining a gym.

Leslie: Okay.

Ron: Let's join one together!

Leslie: Sure! Which gym do you want to join?

Ron: I'm not sure. I want to exercise, but I want a fun workout.

Leslie: Do you like rock climbing?

Ron: I don't know. I have never gone rock climbing.

Leslie: A new rock-climbing gym opened up last week.

Ron: That's cool! Do I have to be good at rock climbing to join?

Leslie: No, you don't. Anyone can join.

Ron: How much is the membership?

Leslie: I think the membership is about $30 a month. Also, the first week is free!

Ron: That's amazing! I didn't know you liked rock climbing.

Leslie: I do! Should we join the rock-climbing gym?

Ron: Okay! Do I need rock climbing shoes?

Leslie: No. You can wear sneakers.

Ron: Do I need special clothes?

Leslie: No, you don't. You can wear normal exercise clothes.

Ron: Okay. This is exciting!

Leslie: It is! Are you ready to go?

Ron: Yeah, let's do it!

23

파리 여행

-

OUR TRIP TO PARIS (A1)

레이첼: 안녕, 세사르!

세사르: 안녕, 어떻게 지냈어? 휴가 사진을 봤어! 정말 멋져 보였어!

레이첼: 멋졌어! 집에 오고 싶지 않았어.

세사르: 당연해. 넌 멋진 걸 정말 많이 했더라! 나는 루브르 박물관과 몽마르트르 사진이 정말 좋았어.

레이첼: 고마워. 여행에서 사진을 오백 장 정도 찍었어. 몇 장만 소셜 미디어에 올렸는데, 사진 전부를 앨범으로 만들 거야. 와서 봐.

세사르: 그러고 싶어! 음식도 너무 맛있어 보여. 너무 부럽다.

레이첼: 이런. 나는 천국에 있었어. 내가 와인이랑 치즈 너무 좋아하는 거 알지.

세사르: 와인 좀 가져왔어?

레이첼: 가방에 넣을 자리가 없었어! 네가 사진 구경하러 와서 좀 마시면 되겠다.

세사르: 좋아! 현지인들은 친절했어?

레이첼: 응. 대부분 너무 착했어.

세사르: 어디에 머물렀어?

레이첼: 우리는 십일 번 어란디스먼트에 머물렀어.

세사르: 십일 번 어...뭐?

레이첼: 하하, 어란디스먼트. 동네 같은 거야.

세사르: 아, 멋지다. 어땠어?

레이첼: 굉장했어. 우리 동네에 괜찮은 식당들이 있었어.

세사르: 음, 빨리 너의 여행에 대해 더 듣고 싶어!

레이첼: 응, 곧 사진 보여줄게!

OUR TRIP TO PARIS

Rachelle: Hi, Cesar!

Cesar: Hey, how are you? I saw the pictures of your vacation! It looked amazing!

Rachelle: It was! I didn't want to come home.

Cesar: I'm not surprised. You did so many cool things! I loved your pictures of the Louvre and Montmartre.

Rachelle: Thanks. I took about five hundred pictures on the trip. I only put some of them on social media, but I will make an album with all the photos. You can come over and look at it.

Cesar: I would love to! The food looked so good, too. I'm so jealous.

Rachelle: Oh my gosh. I was in heaven. You know I love wine and cheese.

Cesar: Did you bring me some wine?

Rachelle: I didn't have room in my suitcase! But you can have some when you come over and look at the pictures.

Cesar: Great! Were the local people friendly?

Rachelle: Yes. Most people were super nice.

Cesar: Where did you stay?

Rachelle: We stayed in the 11th arrondissement.

Cesar: The 11th a-what?

Rachelle: Ha ha, arrondissement. They're like neighborhoods.

Cesar: Oh, cool. How was it?

Rachelle: It was awesome. There were great restaurants in our neighborhood.

Cesar: Well, I can't wait to hear more about your trip!

Rachelle: Yes, I'll show you pictures soon!

24

너무 덥다

-

IT'S TOO HOT (A1)

칼라: 으악, 나는 여름이 싫어.

장웨이: 왜?

칼라: 너무 더워.

장웨이: 맞아. 우리 도시는 특히 더워.

칼라: 핀란드로 이사하고 싶어.

장웨이: 하하, 진짜?

칼라: 음, 응. 근데 나 핀란드어 할 줄 몰라. 그래서 아마 나는 캐나다 북부로 이사할 거야.

장웨이: 정말 아름다울 거야.

칼라: 응. 그래서, 넌 어떤 계절을 제일 좋아해?

장웨이: 사실 난 여름이 제일 좋아.

칼라: 진짜?

장웨이: 응. 하지만 너무 더울 때는 쇼핑몰이나 커피숍 같이 에어컨이 있는 곳에서 시간을 보내.

칼라: 나는 쇼핑몰에 오래 있으면 돈을 다 써버려서 자주는 가지 않으려고 해!

장웨이: 하하, 사실이야. 난 쇼핑몰에 갈 때 신용 카드를 집에 두고 와, 그러면 내가 가진 현금만 사용할 수 있으니까.

칼라: 우와. 그거 정말 좋은 생각이다. 나도 그렇게 해야지.

장웨이: 응, 네가 캐나다에 살 때 캐나다 달러를 쇼핑몰에 가져가면 돼. 덥지도 않고 돈도 많이 절약할 거야!

칼라: 이 아이디어 점점 더 괜찮게 들리는데! 고마워, 장웨이! 하하.

장웨이: 고맙기는! 너보러 캐나다에 가도 될까?

칼라: 물론이지! 네가 원하는 만큼 우리 집에 지내도 돼.

장웨이: 최고야!

IT'S TOO HOT

Carla: Ugh, I don't like the summer.

Zhang-wei: Why not?

Carla: It's too hot.

Zhang-wei: Yeah. It's especially hot in our city.

Carla: I want to move to Finland.

Zhang-wei: Ha ha, really?

Carla: Well, yes. But I don't speak Finnish. So maybe I'll move to northern Canada.

Zhang-wei: I'm sure it's beautiful.

Carla: Yep. So, what's your favorite season?

Zhang-wei: I love the summer, actually.

Carla: Really?

Zhang-wei: Yes. But when it's too hot I just hang out somewhere with air conditioning, like the mall or a coffee shop.

Carla: I try not to go to the mall so much, because whenever I'm there for a long time, I spend all my money!

Zhang-wei: Ha ha, true. I leave my credit cards at home when I go to the mall, so I can't spend more than the cash I bring with me.

Carla: Oh, wow. That's a really good idea. I think I will do that.

Zhang-wei: Yeah, when you live in Canada, you can take your Canadian dollars to the mall. You won't be hot *and* you will save a lot of money!

Carla: This idea is sounding better and better! Thanks, Zhang-wei! Ha ha.

Zhang-wei: No problem! Can I visit you in Canada?

Carla: Of course! You can stay at my place as long as you would like.

Zhang-wei: Great!

25

수면 방식

-

SLEEPING STYLES (A1)

이리나: 안녕하세요, 웨스 씨. 좋아 보이시네요! 머리 잘랐어요?

웨스: 어, 고마워요! 아니요, 안 잘랐어요. 잠을 너무 잘 잤어요. 그래서 제가 달라 보이는 걸까요?

이리나: 네, 아마도요! 푹 쉰 것처럼 보여요!

웨스: 와, 잠도 충분히 잤는데 괜찮아 보이기까지 한다고요? 최고의 날이네요.

이리나: 잠을 좀 잤다니 제가 기쁘네요. 보통 몇 시간 주무세요?

웨스: 다섯 시간에서 여섯 시간 정도요. 요즘 너무 바빠서 잠을 잘 못 잤어요.

이리나: 네, 최근에 새로운 일을 시작했죠, 그렇죠?

웨스: 네. 그리고 첫 월급을 받으면 새 매트리스를 사기로 했었어요. 그리고 그 매트리스가 정말 좋아요!

이리나: 아, 진짜요? 왜 좋아하시나요?

웨스: 부드러움과 단단함의 완벽한 조합이에요. 정말 편해요. 그리고 베개도 새로 샀어요.

이리나: 정말 좋네요. 제 매트리스는 너무 낡았어요! 그래서 그런지 잠을 잘 못 자요.

웨스: 아마도요! 새 매트리스가 잠을 잘 자도록 도울 수 있는지 몰랐어요.

이리나: 와. 아마 저도 매트리스를 새로 사야 할까 봐요!

웨스: 강력히 추천해요!

SLEEPING STYLES

Irina: Hi, Wes. You look great! Did you get a haircut?

Wes: Oh, thanks! No, I didn't. I slept really well. Maybe that's why I look different?

Irina: Yes, maybe! You look well-rested!

Wes: Wow, I got enough sleep *and* I look good? This is the best day ever.

Irina: Well I'm happy you got some sleep. How many hours of sleep do you usually get?

Wes: Maybe five or six hours. I am so busy these days, so it's hard to sleep.

Irina: Yeah, you just started a new job, right?

Wes: Yes. And I decided to buy a new mattress with my first paycheck. And I love it!

Irina: Oh, really? Why do you love it?

Wes: It's the perfect combination of soft and firm. It's so comfortable. And I got some new pillows too.

Irina: That sounds amazing. My mattress is so old! Maybe that's why I don't sleep very well.

Wes: Maybe! I didn't realize that a new mattress can help you sleep so well.

Irina: Wow. Maybe I should buy a new mattress!

Wes: I highly recommend it!

26

가게에 상품 반품하기

-

RETURNING AN ITEM TO THE STORE (A2)

디브야: 안녕하세요, 어떻게 도와드릴까요?

미하일: 이 셔츠를 반품하고 싶어요.

디브야: 알겠습니다. 셔츠에 무슨 문제가 있었나요?

미하일: 네. 오른쪽 소매에 작은 구멍이 있는 걸 사고 나서 확인했어요.

디브야: 알겠습니다. 유감이네요. 영수증 갖고 계신가요?

미하일: 아니요. 그게 문제에요. 영수증을 버렸어요.

디브야: 아, 그렇군요.. 음, 아직 가격표가 붙어 있어서 다행이네요. 보통 반품할 때 영수증이 필요해요. 하지만 셔츠에 문제가 있었고 가격표가 아직 붙어 있으니 반품을 해드리겠습니다.

미하일: 정말 감사합니다.

디브야: 천만에요. 불편을 드려 죄송합니다.

미하일: 괜찮습니다. 저는 이 가게가 좋기도 하고, 이곳에 계신 분들께서 고객 서비스가 항상 좋으세요.

디브야: 감사합니다! 이 셔츠를 구매하실 때 사용한 신용카드 갖고 계신가요?

미하일: 네, 여기 있습니다.

디브야: 감사합니다. 카드를 여기에 넣어주시면 됩니다.

미하일: 알겠습니다.

디브야: 그리고 거기 화면에 사인 부탁드립니다.

미하일: 돈은 다시 제 카드로 들어오나요?

디브야: 네. 24 시간 이내에 환불을 받으실 거예요. 영수증 필요하세요?

미하일: 네, 부탁합니다! 이번에는 버리지 않을게요.

디브야: 하하, 좋아요! 좋은 하루 보내세요!

미하일: 감사합니다. 좋은 하루 보내세요.

RETURNING AN ITEM TO THE STORE

Divya: Hello, how can I help you?

Mikhail: I would like to return this shirt.

Divya: Okay. Was something wrong with the shirt?

Mikhail: Yes. I noticed after I bought it that there is a small hole on the right sleeve.

Divya: I see. I'm sorry to hear about that. Do you have the receipt?

Mikhail: No. That's the problem. I threw away the receipt.

Divya: Oh, I see. Well, the price tag is still on it, so that's good. Usually we require the receipt for returns. But because there was a problem with the shirt and the price tag is still on it, we will accept the return.

Mikhail: Thanks so much.

Divya: Of course. I'm sorry for the inconvenience.

Mikhail: It's fine. I like this store and you guys always have good customer service.

Divya: Thank you! Do you have the credit card that you used to buy the shirt?

Mikhail: Yes, here it is.

Divya: Thank you. You can insert the card here.

Mikhail: Okay.

Divya: And sign right there on the screen.

Mikhail: Will the money go back onto my card?

Divya: Yes. You will get a refund within twenty-four hours. Would you like a receipt?

Mikhail: Yes, please! And this time I won't throw it away.

Divya: Ha ha, good! Have a good day!

Mikhail: Thanks; you too.

27

식품점에서

-

AT THE GROCERY STORE (A2)

서연: 우리 필요한 게 뭐야?

맥스: 상추, 토마토, 양파, 사과, 요구르트, 머스터드 소스...

서연: 과일과 채소부터 시작하자. 토마토는 몇 개 필요해?

맥스: 네 개.

서연: 알았어.

맥스: 여기 토마토 네 개 있어.

서연: 그건 덜 익었어.

맥스: 아, 알았어. 이건 어때?

서연: 그건 괜찮네. 양파는 몇 개 필요해?

맥스: 한 개만.

서연: 빨간색 아니면 노란색?

맥스: 음... 빨간색.

서연: 그리고 어떤 상추 필요해?

맥스: 로메인으로 사자.

서연: 알았어. 아, 당근하고 셀러리도 좀 사자.

맥스: 집에 셀러리 있어.

서연: 있어?

맥스: 응.

서연: 아직 싱싱해?

맥스: 그런 것 같아.

서연: 좋아. 저기 사과 있다.

맥스: 내가 몇 개 가져올게.

서연: 목요일하고 금요일 저녁으로 먹을 것 좀 사야겠지?

맥스: 응, 뭘 사야 할까?

서연: 파스타와 닭고기 어때?

맥스: 어떤 파스타?

서연: 팬네?

맥스: 좋아, 그럼. 어떤 소스로 만들까?

서연: 매운 토마토 소스로 하자.

맥스: 오오, 좋은 생각이야. 닭고가는 어떻게 할까?

서연: 사워크림, 파르메산 치즈, 그리고 몇 가지 간단한 양념으로 만드는 닭 가슴살 조리법을 봤어. 만들기가 매우 쉽더라고.

맥스: 좋은데! 그거 만들자.

서연: 완벽해! 재료를 사자.

AT THE GROCERY STORE

Seo-yeon: What do we need?

Max: Lettuce, tomatoes, onions, apples, yogurt, mustard...

Seo-yeon: Let's start with the fruits and veggies. How many tomatoes do we need?

Max: Four.

Seo-yeon: Okay.

Max: Here are four tomatoes.

Seo-yeon: That one isn't ripe.

Max: Oh, I see. What about this one?

Seo-yeon: That one's good. How many onions do we need?

Max: Just one.

Seo-yeon: Red or yellow?

Max: Umm... red.

Seo-yeon: And what kind of lettuce?

Max: Let's get romaine.

Seo-yeon: All right. Oh, let's get some carrots and celery too.

Max: We already have celery at home.

Seo-yeon: We do?

Max: Yeah.

Seo-yeon: And it's still good?

Max: I think so.

Seo-yeon: Great. There are the apples.

Max: I'll get a few.

Seo-yeon: Should we get stuff for dinner on Thursday and Friday?

Max: Yeah, what should we get?

Seo-yeon: Maybe pasta and some chicken?

Max: What kind of pasta?

Seo-yeon: Penne?

Max: Okay, sure. What kind of sauce should we make?

Seo-yeon: Let's do a spicy tomato sauce.

Max: Ooh, that sounds good. And what should we do with the chicken?

Seo-yeon: I saw a recipe for chicken breasts with sour cream, Parmesan cheese, and a few simple seasonings. It's very easy to make.

Max: Sounds good! Let's make that.

Seo-yeon: Perfect! Let's get the ingredients.

28

아파트 찾기

-

LOOKING FOR APARTMENTS (A2)

리나: 우리가 살 아파트를 찾아야 해.

비센티: 알았어. 어떤 동네를 살펴봐야 할까?

리나: 노스 파크, 힐크레스트, 노멀 하이츠에 집중해야 할 것 같아.

비센티: 사우스 파크는 어때?

리나: 내 생각에 사우스 파크는 좀 너무 비싼 것 같아. 웹 사이트 몇 개 살펴보자.

비센티: 좋은 생각이야.

리나: 이 아파트를 봐. 큰 거실 하나에 큰 방이 딸려 있어. 한 달에 천삼백 달러 밖에 안돼.

비센티: 싸다. 어디에 있는 거야?

리나: 노스 파크에 있어. 그리고 그 아파트 단지에는 수영장이 있어!

비센티: 오, 좋다! 반려견도 허용된대?

리나: 아, 이런. 그걸 잊어버렸네. 우리는 개가 있지!

비센티: 어떻게 그걸 잊어버릴 수 있어?!

리나: 몰라. 흠... 여기에 다른 아파트가 있어. 힐크레스트에 있고 반려견을 허용해. 그런데 수영장은 없어.

비센티: 괜찮아. 우리는 수영장이 필요 없어. 집세는 얼마야?

리나: 한 달에 천사백오십 달러야.

비센티: 그건 좀 비싸네.

리나: 응, 맞아. 그런데 정말 좋은 지역이고 아파트에 두 개의 주차 공간이 있어.

비센티: 오, 그거 좋다. 그 동네에서는 주차하기 어려울 수도 있어!

리나: 맞아, 그건 사실이야.

비센티: 연락해 볼까?

리나: 응, 그래야지. 내가 지금 이메일을 보낼게.

비센티: 좋아! 그래도 아파트를 더 찾아보자.

리나: 응, 좋은 생각이야.

LOOKING FOR APARTMENTS

Lina: We need to look for an apartment.

Vicente: Okay. What neighborhoods should we look in?

Lina: I think we should focus on North Park, Hillcrest, and Normal Heights.

Vicente: What about South Park?

Lina: I think South Park is a little too expensive. Let's look at some websites.

Vicente: Good idea.

Lina: Look at this apartment. It's a one-bedroom with a big living room. And it's only $1,300 a month.

Vicente: That's cheap. Where is it?

Lina: It's in North Park. And the apartment complex has a pool!

Vicente: Oh, nice! Does it allow dogs?

Lina: Oh, oops. I forgot about that. We have a dog!

Vicente: How could you forget that?!

Lina: I don't know. Hmm... here is another apartment. This one is in Hillcrest and it allows dogs. But it doesn't have a pool.

Vicente: That's okay. We don't need a pool. How much is the rent?

Lina: It's $1,450 a month.

Vicente: That's a little expensive.

Lina: Yeah, it is. But the area is really nice and the apartment has two parking spaces too.

Vicente: Oh, that's good. Parking can be difficult in that neighborhood!

Lina: Yes, that's true.

Vicente: Should we contact them?

Lina: Yes, we should. I'll send them an email now.

Vicente: Great! But let's keep looking for more apartments.

Lina: Yes, good idea.

29

건강식
-
EATING HEALTHILY (A2)

캐서린: 전 더 건강하게 먹고 싶어요.

그레그: 하지만 캐서린 씨는 이미 건강한 음식을 먹고 있잖아요, 그렇지 않나요?

캐서린: 말도 안 돼요! 저는 정크 푸드를 너무 많이 먹어요. 또 과일이랑 채소를 충분히 먹지 않고요.

그레그: 캐서린 씨 젊잖아요. 나중에 나이가 들었을 때 더 건강한 음식을 먹기 시작해도 돼요.

캐서린: 아니요, 지금 시작하는 것이 중요해요.

그레그: 알았어요. 그래서 뭘 먹을 거예요?

캐서린: 음, 아침으로 오트밀이나 과일, 또는 요구르트를 먹을 거예요. 그리고 차도 좀 마시고요.

그레그: 따분하겠어요.

캐서린: 맛있는 과일이랑 요구르트가 얼마나 많은데요! 오트밀은 약간 따분하긴 하지만 전 거기에 과일과 흑설탕을 넣어요. 오트밀을 더 맛있게 만들거든요.

그레그: 그렇군요. 점심으로는 뭘 먹을 거예요?

캐서린: 샐러드, 채소, 그리고 아마 밥도 조금 먹을 거예요.

그레그: 샐러드를 먹고 나면 배가 부를까요?

캐서린: 네, 양이 많으면요.

그레그: 그리고 저녁으로는 뭘 먹을 거예요?

캐서린: 채소, 닭고기, 콩, 샐러드... 같은 것이요.

그레그: 오, 저 닭고기 좋아해요!

캐서린: 저도요.

그레그: 흠... 저도 이 건강한 식단을 짧게 시도해 볼래요.

캐서린: 정말요? 하지만 그레그 씨는 건강한 음식이 대체로 따분하다고 생각하잖아요.

그레그: 네, 하지만 캐서린 씨에게서 영감을 받았어요. 저도 캐서린 씨처럼 건강해지고 싶어요.

캐서린: 하하! 좋아요... 우리 함께 건강해져요!

그레그: 야호!

EATING HEALTHILY

Catherine: I want to eat more healthy foods.

Greg: But you already eat healthy foods, right?

Catherine: No way! I eat so much junk food. And I don't eat enough fruits and vegetables.

Greg: But you're young. You can start eating more healthy foods later when you're older.

Catherine: No, it's important to start now.

Greg: Okay. So, what will you eat?

Catherine: Well, for breakfast I will eat oatmeal or fruit or yogurt. And maybe drink some tea.

Greg: That sounds boring.

Catherine: There are many delicious fruits and yogurts! Oatmeal is a little boring, but I add fruit and brown sugar to it. That makes it tastier.

Greg: I see. What will you eat for lunch?

Catherine: Salad, vegetables, maybe some rice.

Greg: Will you feel full after eating salad?

Catherine: Yes, if it is big.

Greg: And what will you eat for dinner?

Catherine: Vegetables, chicken, beans, salad… things like that.

Greg: Oh, I like chicken!

Catherine: Me too.

Greg: Hmm… maybe I'll try this healthy diet for a short time.

Catherine: Really? But you think most healthy food is boring.

Greg: Yeah, but you are inspiring me. I want to be healthy like you.

Catherine: Ha ha wow! Okay… let's get healthy together!

Greg: Woohoo!

30

결혼식 계획

-

PLANNING A WEDDING (A2)

사라: 우리 결혼식이 너무 기대돼!

패트릭: 나도!

사라: 우리는 결혼식까지 일 년 남았으니까 지금부터 계획을 세우기 시작해야 해.

패트릭: 일 년이면 많이 남은 거야!

사라: 그렇지 않아! 시간이 엄청 빨리 지나갈 거야.

패트릭: 흠, 알겠어. 그럼 우리 먼저 어떤 것부터 해야 해?

사라: 결혼식을 얼마나 크게 할 건지 이야기 해보자. 몇 명을 초대해야 할까?

패트릭: 흠, 아마 이백 명 정도 되려나?

사라: 이백 명?! 너무 많은 걸!

패트릭: 진짜? 그게 보통인데, 그렇지 않아?

사라: 나는 백 명이나 백오십 명이 좀 더 보통이라고 생각해.

패트릭: 알았어. 백오십 명 정도 될 거야.

사라: 그리고 어디서 결혼하고 싶어? 해변? 공원? 호텔?

패트릭: 나는 항상 해변에서 결혼하고 싶었어.

사라: 나도 마찬가지야! 봤지? 이래서 내가 너를 사랑한다니까. 어떤 음식을 대접할까?

패트릭: 나는 스테이크와 초밥을 대접했으면 해!

사라: 스테이크와 초밥? 그건 비쌀 것 같은데!

패트릭: 알았어... 그럼 그냥 스테이크만?

사라: 흠... 그건 나중에 이야기하자. 음악은 어떻게 할까?

패트릭: 난 우리가 밤새 춤출 수 있도록 디제이가 있었으면 좋겠어!

사라: 네가 춤추는 걸 네 친구들과 가족 모두에게 정말 보여주고 싶어?

패트릭: 하하, 무슨 소리야?

사라: 음, 나는 너의 멋진 마음과 성격이 좋아서 너와 결혼하는 거야, 너의 춤 실력은 말고!

패트릭: 너무해!

PLANNING A WEDDING

Sara: I'm so excited for our wedding!

Patrick: Me too!

Sara: We only have a year to plan it, so we should start planning now.

Patrick: A year is a long time!

Sara: Not really! It will go very fast.

Patrick: Hmm, yeah. So, what should we do first?

Sara: Let's talk about the size of the wedding. How many people should we invite?

Patrick: Hmm, maybe two hundred?

Sara: Two hundred?! That's so many!

Patrick: Really? That's normal, right?

Sara: I think one hundred or one hundred fifty is more normal.

Patrick: All right. Maybe one hundred fifty.

Sara: And where do you want to get married? The beach? A park? A hotel?

Patrick: I have always wanted to get married at the beach.

Sara: Me too! See? This is why I love you. What kind of food should we serve?

Patrick: I want steak and sushi!

Sara: Steak and sushi? I think that will be expensive!

Patrick: Okay… maybe just steak?

Sara: Hmmm… let's talk about that later. What about music?

Patrick: I want a DJ so we can dance all night!

Sara: Are you sure you want all your friends and family to see you dance?

Patrick: Ha ha, what are you saying?

Sara: Well, I'm marrying you for your wonderful heart and personality, not for your dancing skills!

Patrick: Ouch!

31

나는 머리를 잘라야 해

-

I NEED A HAIRCUT (A2)

예세니아: 나 머리 잘라야 해.

메튜: 머리 괜찮은데.

예세니아: 맞아, 나쁘지는 않은데 너무 길어.

메튜: 얼마나 자를 거야?

예세니아: 몇 인치만.

메튜: 그렇게 많이는 안 자르네. 어짜피 돈 내고 자르는 거 좀 더 확실한 변화를 줘 봐.

예세니아: 근데 난 스타일을 많이 바꾸고 싶지 않아!

메튜: 그러면 왜 자르려고 하는데?

예세니아: 왜냐하면 머리카락을 건강하게 유지하고 싶기 때문이야.

메튜: 아, 알겠어. 그래서 비용이 얼마 정도 들어?

예세니아: 보통 사십오 달러 정도 들어.

메튜: 사십오 달러! 너무 비싸다!

예세니아: 이 도시에서는 그게 여자 머리를 자르는 데 드는 평균 비용이야.

메튜: 와, 난 남자라서 다행이다. 머리 염색하는데는 얼마나 들어?

예세니아: 네가 무엇을 하냐에 따라 다르지만, 백 달러 정도 들어.

메튜: 백 달러?! 사람들이 머리하는 데 돈을 그만큼 쓰는 게 믿어지지가 않아.

예세니아: 맞아, 비싸. 하지만 내 머리가 예쁘면, 난 행복해.

메튜: 뭐, 네가 행복하면, 나도 행복해. 그러면 이 머리 스타일은 우리 모두에게 좋은 거네!

예세니아: 하하. 알았어, 지금 예약을 할게.

메튜: 좋아!

I NEED A HAIRCUT

Yesenia: I need to get a haircut.

Matthew: I think your hair looks fine.

Yesenia: Yeah, it doesn't look bad, but it's too long.

Matthew: How much will you cut?

Yesenia: Just a couple inches.

Matthew: That's not very much. If you're already paying for a cut, you should do something more dramatic.

Yesenia: But I don't want to change it very much!

Matthew: So why do you want to cut it?

Yesenia: Because I want to keep my hair healthy.

Matthew: Oh, I see. So how much will it cost?

Yesenia: It usually costs around forty-five dollars.

Matthew: Forty-five dollars! That's so expensive!

Yesenia: That's the average cost for women's haircuts in this city.

Matthew: Wow, I'm glad I'm a guy. How much does it cost to dye your hair?

Yesenia: It depends on what you do, but around one hundred dollars.

Matthew: One hundred dollars?! I can't believe how much some people spend on their hair.

Yesenia: Yeah, it's a lot. But when my hair looks good, I'm happy.

Matthew: Well, when you're happy, I'm happy. So, this haircut is good for both of us!

Yesenia: Ha ha. All right, I will make the appointment now.

Matthew: Great!

32

수족관에 가기

-

GOING TO AN AQUARIUM (A2)

카일리: 오늘 수족관에 가자.

대런: 좋은 생각이야! 어떤 수족관?

카일리: 선샤인 수족관. 새로 생겼어.

대런: 아, 진짜? 좋아. 몇 시에 출발해야 해?

카일리: 아홉 시 반에 출발하자. 오픈 전에 도착하고 싶어.

대런: 왜 이렇게 일찍 가고 싶은 거야?

카일리: 왜냐하면 인기 있는 수족관이라 사람이 많이 올 거라서 그래.

대런: 알았어. 표를 온라인에서 살까, 아니면 수족관에서 살까?

카일리: 온라인이나 수족관 둘 다 가능한데, 온라인으로 사면 이 달러가 더 저렴해.

대런: 아, 알겠어. 온라인에서 표를 사자. 내가 할게. 웹 사이트 주소가 뭐야?

카일리: www.sunshinesquarium.com

대런: 알았어. 일반 성인 표를 사야 할까, 아니면 단체 성인 표를 사야 할까?

카일리: 그냥 일반 성인 표.

대런: 좋아. 내 직불 카드를 사용할게.

카일리: 좋아, 고마워! 내가 점심을 살게.

(수족관에서)

대런: 어디부터 갈까?

카일리: 해파리 보자!

대런: 알았어! 해파리는 정말 멋있어. 그런데 약간 무섭기도 해.

카일리: 맞아. 나는 해파리를 수족관에서 보는 게 좋아. 바다에서 말고!

대런: 하하, 나도.

카일리: 저것 좀 봐! 엄청나게 커!

대런: 우와!

카일리: 다음에는 무엇을 볼까?

대런: 문어를 보자!

카일리: 윽... 나는 문어가 싫어. 너는 문어 보러 가. 나는 가오리를 보러 갈게.

대런: 좋아. 있다가 보자!

GOING TO AN AQUARIUM

Kylie: Let's go to the aquarium today.

Darren: That's a good idea! Which one?

Kylie: Sunshine Aquarium. It's new.

Darren: Oh, really? Cool. What time should we leave?

Kylie: Let's leave at nine thirty. I want to arrive before they open.

Darren: Why do you want to arrive so early?

Kylie: Because the aquarium is popular and many people will be there.

Darren: Okay. Do we buy tickets online or at the aquarium?

Kylie: We can buy tickets online or at the aquarium, but it's two dollars cheaper if we buy them online.

Darren: Oh, I see. Let's buy the tickets online. I will do it. What's the website?

Kylie: www.sunshinesquarium.com

Darren: All right. Should we buy the regular adult tickets or the adult tickets with the tour?

Kylie: Just the regular adult tickets.

Darren: Cool. I will use my debit card.

Kylie: Great, thanks! I will buy lunch.

(At the aquarium)

Darren: Where should we go first?

Kylie: Let's see the jellyfish!

Darren: Okay! Jellyfish are so cool. But they are also a little scary.

Kylie: I agree. I like to see them in an aquarium. Not in the ocean!

Darren: Ha ha, me too.

Kylie: Look at that one! It's so big!

Darren: Wow!

Kylie: What should we see next?

Darren: Let's look at the octopuses!

Kylie: Eww… I hate octopuses. You can go there. I will go check out the stingrays.

Darren: That works for me. See you soon!

33

이 커피는 뜨겁지 않아요

-

THIS COFFEE IS NOT HOT (A2)

신시아: 실례합니다. 이 커피는 별로 뜨겁지 않아요. 다른 걸로 주실 수 있으신가요?

빅터: 아, 이상하네요. 제가 방금 내렸거든요.

신시아: 기계에 문제가 있는 것이 아닐까요?

빅터: 그럴 리가 없어요. 하지만 물론이죠, 제가 다른 걸 만들어 드릴게요.

신시아: 감사합니다! 아마 저만 그런 게 아닐까요? 저는 아주 뜨거운 커피를 좋아해요.

빅터: 아, 진짜요?

신시아: 네. 저는 뜨거운 커피가 더 맛있어요!

빅터: 흥미롭네요. 전 사실 아이스 커피를 더 선호해요.

신시아: 저도 아이스 커피를 좋아하지만, 밖이 더울 때만 그래요.

빅터: 네. 제가 좀 이상해요.

신시아: 하하. 글쎄요, 저희 둘 다 이상할지도 몰라요.

빅터: 네, 아마도요! 여기 새 커피가 있습니다. 더 뜨겁게 만드려고 했어요.

신시아: 어머나! 뜨겁네요! 사실 이건 너무 뜨거운 것 같아요! 몇 분 기다렸다가 마셔야겠어요.

빅터: 네, 조심하세요. 손님이 화상 입는 것을 원치 않아요.

신시아: 저도요. 그런데 맛이 좋네요. 어떤 종류의 커피인가요?

빅터: 과테말라산이에요. 맛있죠?

신시아: 네, 매우 맛있어요. 좋아요, 커피가 식었어요. 이제 마실 수 있겠어요.

빅터: 좋네요! 총 사 달러 오 센트입니다.

신시아: 여기 오 달러 있습니다.

빅터: 감사합니다. 거스름돈 구십오 센트입니다. 뜨거운 커피 맛있게 드시고 좋은 하루 보내세요!

신시아: 감사합니다! 그리고 새 커피를 만들어 주셔서 감사합니다.

빅터: 천만에요.

THIS COFFEE IS NOT HOT

Cynthia: Excuse me. This coffee is not very hot. Can I get another one?

Victor: Oh, that's weird. I just made it.

Cynthia: Maybe there is a problem with the machine?

Victor: I don't think so. But sure, I can make you another coffee.

Cynthia: Thank you! Maybe it's just me? I like very hot coffee.

Victor: Oh, really?

Cynthia: Yes. Hot coffee just tastes better to me!

Victor: Interesting. I actually prefer iced coffee.

Cynthia: I like iced coffee, but only when it's hot outside.

Victor: Yeah. I'm kind of strange.

Cynthia: Ha ha. Well, maybe we are both strange.

Victor: Yes, maybe! Here is your new coffee. I tried to make it extra hot.

Cynthia: Oh wow! This is hot! I think it's actually too hot! I will wait a couple minutes to drink it.

Victor: Yes, please be careful. I don't want you to burn yourself.

Cynthia: Me neither. I like the flavor, though. What kind of coffee is this?

Victor: It's from Guatemala. It's good, right?

Cynthia: Yes, it's very good. Okay, the coffee has cooled down. I can drink it now.

Victor: Good! So, your total will be $4.05.

Cynthia: Here is five dollars.

Victor: Thanks. Your change is $.95. Enjoy your hot coffee and have a good day!

Cynthia: Thanks! And thank you for making me a new coffee.

Victor: No problem.

34

새해 전날 밤 계획

-

NEW YEAR'S EVE PLANS (A2)

롭: 안녕, 핼리! 새해 전날 밤에 뭐할 거야?

핼리: 안녕, 롭! 아직 모르겠어. 너는 뭐할 거야?

롭: 나는 친구 집에 가서 파티 할 거야. 나랑 같이 갈래?

핼리: 물론! 네 친구 누구? 집이 어디야?

롭: 내 친구 라이언인데, 같이 일하는 동료야. 얘네 집이 바닷가 근처에 있어.

핼리: 오, 좋다! 사람들은 얼마나 많이 와?

롭: 스무 명에서 서른 명쯤 될 것 같아.

핼리: 우와, 많다.

롭: 응, 라이언이 친구가 많아! 하하.

핼리: 그런 것 같아. 내가 뭐 가져갈까?

롭: 괜찮다면, 사람들이랑 같이 나눠 먹을 간식이나 마실 것 좀 가지고 가면 될 것 같아.

핼리: 그렇게 할게. 마실 건 어떤 거 가져갈까?

롭: 아마 맥주나 와인?

핼리: 알았어! 우와, 너 봐서 기쁘다! 새해 전날 밤에 계획이 없어서 슬펐거든!

롭: 아이고, 나도 기뻐! 사실 작년 새해 전날 밤에 아무것도 하지 않았거든. 이번 해에는 뭔가를 할 수 있어서 기뻐.

핼리: 정말? 왜 아무것도 안했어?

롭: 나 정말 아팠거든!

핼리: 오, 저런! 끔찍하네.

롭: 응. 괜찮아. 적어도 돈은 아꼈지.

핼리: 하하. 진짜네! 그럼, 파티에서 보자!

롭: 응, 거기서 봐!

NEW YEAR'S EVE PLANS

Rob: Hey, Hallie! What will you do for New Year's Eve?

Hallie: Hi, Rob! I don't know yet. What will you do?

Rob: I will go to my friend's house for a party. Do you want to come with me?

Hallie: Sure! Who is your friend? Where is the house?

Rob: It's my friend Ryan. I work with him. His house is near the beach.

Hallie: Oh, cool! How many people will be there?

Rob: I think twenty or thirty.

Hallie: Wow, that's a lot.

Rob: Yeah, Ryan has a lot of friends! Ha ha.

Hallie: It sounds like it. Do I need to bring anything?

Rob: If you want, you can bring some drinks or snacks for people to share.

Hallie: I can do that. What kind of drinks should I bring?

Rob: Maybe some beer or wine?

Hallie: Okay! Wow, I'm glad I saw you! I didn't have any plans for New Year's Eve and I was sad!

Rob: Aww, I'm glad too! Actually, last year I didn't do anything for New Year's, so I'm happy I can do something this year.

Hallie: Really? Why didn't you do anything?

Rob: I was really sick!

Hallie: Oh no! That's terrible.

Rob: Yeah. It's okay. At least I saved money.

Hallie: Ha ha. True! Well, I'll see you at the party!

Rob: Yep, see you there!

35

지난 밤 내 꿈

-

MY DREAM LAST NIGHT (A2)

압둘라: 어젯밤에 아주 이상한 꿈을 꿨어!

프란체스카: 진짜? 뭐에 관한 거였는데?

압둘라: 내가 농장에 있었는데 그 농장에 이상한 동물들이 많이 있었어. 염소, 돼지, 소처럼 평범한 동물들도 있었지만, 얼룩말, 캥거루, 심지어 호랑이도 있었어.

프란체스카: 와, 재미있는 농장이네.

압둘라: 응. 그리고 몇몇 얼룩말들은 다른 색깔의 줄무늬를 갖고 있었어. 어떤 것은 파란색, 어떤 것은 보라색이었어. 그리고 몇몇은 무지개 줄무늬를 가지고 있더라고!

프란체스카: 하하, 진짜?

압둘라: 그러고 나서 호랑이가 나에게 말을 했어. 그런데 스페인어로 말을 하더라고.

프란체스카: 스페인어? 뭐라고 이야기했는데?

압둘라: 몰라! 나는 스페인어를 못해!

프란체스카: 아, 맞다. 그럼 호랑이가 스페인어로 말한 건 어떻게 알았어?

압둘라: 흠, 스페인어가 어떻게 들리는 지는 아니까.

프란체스카: 아. 그러고 나서 무슨 일이 있었어?

압둘라: 기억이 안 나.

프란체스카: 항상 이상한 꿈을 꿔?

압둘라: 응, 그런데 이렇게 이상하지는 않아.

프란체스카: 꿈에 어떤 의미가 있다고 생각해?

압둘라: 가끔. 너는 어때?

프란체스카: 그런 것 같아. 아마 네가 네 삶에서 더 많은 친구를 필요로 하는 것일지도 몰라.

압둘라: 나는 친구가 많아!

프란체스카: 아마 네 친구들이 지루해서 네가 더 재미있는 친구들을 원하는 것일지도 몰라. 무지개 줄무늬 얼룩말처럼.

압둘라: 하하, 그런가!

MY DREAM LAST NIGHT

Abdullah: I had a very weird dream last night!

Francesca: Really? What was it about?

Abdullah: I was on a farm and there were a lot of strange animals. There were normal animals like goats, pigs, and cows, but then there were also zebras, kangaroos, and even a tiger.

Francesca: Wow, that's an interesting farm.

Abdullah: Yeah. And some of the zebras had different colored stripes. Some were blue, some were purple. And some were rainbow-striped!

Francesca: Ha ha, really?

Abdullah: And then the tiger talked to me. But it spoke in Spanish.

Francesca: Spanish?? What did it say?

Abdullah: I don't know! I don't speak Spanish!

Francesca: Oh, right. So how do you know it was speaking Spanish?

Abdullah: Well, I know what Spanish sounds like.

Francesca: Oh. Then what happened?

Abdullah: I don't remember.

Francesca: Do you always have weird dreams?

Abdullah: Yeah, but not *this* weird.

Francesca: Do you think dreams mean anything?

Abdullah: Sometimes. What about you?

Francesca: I think so. Maybe you want more friends in your life.

Abdullah: I have a lot of friends!

Francesca: Maybe your friends are boring and you want more interesting friends. Like rainbow-striped zebras.

Abdullah: Ha ha, maybe!

36

학교 갈 준비하기

-

GETTING READY FOR SCHOOL (A2)

그레이스: 크리스토퍼, 일어날 시간이야!

크리스토퍼: 아. 오 분만 더요.

그레이스: 그 말 오 분 전에도 했어. 일어날 시간이야, 크리스토퍼.

크리스토퍼: 아, 알았어요.

그레이스: 가서 이 닦고 옷 입어라.

크리스토퍼: 엄마가 골라준 셔츠 입기 싫어요.

그레이스: 왜?

크리스토퍼: 더 이상 그 셔츠를 좋아하지 않아요.

그레이스: 알았어, 그러면 다른 셔츠를 골라봐.

크리스토퍼: 엄마가 해주실 수 있어요?

그레이스: 아니, 넌 이제 다 컸잖아. 네 셔츠는 네가 골라야지.

크리스토퍼: 알겠어요. 이거 입을게요.

그레이스: 알았어. 준비되면 아침 먹으러 와.

크리스토퍼: 알겠어요.

(십 분 후...)

그레이스: 빨리 먹어. 우리 조금 늦었어.

크리스토퍼: 네, 네. 초콜릿 오즈좀 주시겠어요?

그레이스: 초콜릿 오즈는 주말에만 먹을 수 있는거 알잖아.

크리스토퍼: 하지만 다른 건 먹고 싶지 않은 걸요.

그레이스: 오늘 왜 이렇게 까다롭게 굴어, 크리스토퍼?!

크리스토퍼: 전 까다롭게 굴지 않았어요.

그레이스: 그레놀라 시리얼 먹어.

크리스토퍼: 좋아요.

그레이스: 오늘 햄이나 달걀 샐러드 샌드위치 먹을래?

크리스토퍼: 음... 햄이요.

그레이스: 사과도 꼭 먹어야 해, 알았지?

크리스토퍼: 네, 엄마.

그레이스: 좋아, 갈 시간이야!

GETTING READY FOR SCHOOL

Grace: Honey, it's time to wake up!

Christopher: Ugh. Five more minutes.

Grace: That's what you said five minutes ago. It's time to get up, sweetie.

Christopher: Ugh, okay.

Grace: Go brush your teeth and get dressed.

Christopher: I don't want to wear the shirt you picked out for me.

Grace: Why not?

Christopher: I don't like it anymore.

Grace: Okay, then pick out a different shirt.

Christopher: Can you do it?

Grace: No, you're a big boy now. You can pick out your own shirts.

Christopher: All right. I'll wear this one.

Grace: Okay. Come eat breakfast when you're ready.

Christopher: All right.

(Ten minutes later...)

Grace: You need to eat quickly. We're a little late.

Christopher: Yeah, yeah. Can I have Chocolate O's?

Grace: You know you can only have Chocolate O's on the weekend.

Christopher: But I don't want anything else.

Grace: Why are you being so difficult today, Christopher?!

Christopher: I'm not being difficult.

Grace: Eat the granola cereal.

Christopher: Fine.

Grace: Would you like a ham or egg salad sandwich today?

Christopher: Umm... ham.

Grace: Make sure to eat the apple too, OKAY?

Christopher: Yes, Mom.

Grace: All right, time to go!

37

침대 쇼핑하기

-

SHOPPING FOR A BED (A2)

레나타: 퀸 사이즈와 킹 사이즈 중에 어떤 매트리스를 사야 할까?

니마: 우리 킹 사이즈 매트리스를 사야 돼. 너 잘 때 많이 움직이잖아!

레나타: 에고, 미안!

니마: 괜찮아. 하지만 우리 둘 다 편할 수 있게 이 사이즈를 사는 게 좋을 것 같아.

레나타: 맞아.

니마: 너는 더 부드러운 매트리스를 좋아하지 않아?

레나타: 응. 너도 그렇잖아, 안 그래?

니마: 응. 다행이네!

레나타: 이 매트리스들은 우리가 원하는 가격대 안에 있어.

니마: 응, 한 번 보자.

레나타: 흠... 내 생각에 이건 너무 딱딱한 것 같아. 어떻게 생각해?

니마: 어디 보자. 응... 너무 딱딱해.

레나타: 이건 어때?

니마: 오, 이거 좋다.

레나타: 오, 네 말이 맞아. 이게 좋아. 얼마야?

니마: 약간 비싸지만 매달 나눠서 지불하면 돼.

레나타: 좋다. 그럼, 어떤 종류의 침대 프레임을 사야 할까?

니마: 난 별로 신경 안 써. 나한텐 매트리스가 더 중요해.

레나타: 알았어! 내가 침대 프레임을 고를게. 나는 그 하얀 프레임이 좋아.

니마: 응, 그거 좋다.

레나타: 그리고 가격도 좋아.

니마: 응.

레나타: 음, 침대 쇼핑 쉬운데!

니마: 응, 맞아! 나는 침대 쇼핑을 하루 종일 할 줄 알았어!

레나타: 앗싸! 축하도 할 겸 저녁 먹으러 가자!

니마: 우리 방금 돈을 많이 썼어. 저녁은 집에서 먹어야 할 것 같아.

레나타: 응, 네 말이 맞아. 알았어, 저녁은 집에서 먹자!

SHOPPING FOR A BED

Renata: Should we buy a queen- or king-size mattress?

Nima: We need to get a king-size mattress. You move around a lot when you sleep!

Renata: Oops, sorry!

Nima: It's okay. But I think we should get this size so both of us can be comfortable.

Renata: I agree.

Nima: You like softer mattresses, don't you?

Renata: Yeah. You do too, right?

Nima: Yes. Thank goodness!

Renata: These mattresses here are in our price range.

Nima: Yeah, let's try them out.

Renata: Hmm... I think this one is too hard. What do you think?

Nima: Let me see. Yeah... that's too hard.

Renata: What about this one?

Nima: Oh, this one is nice.

Renata: Ooh, you're right. I like this one. How much is it?

Nima: It's a little expensive, but we can make monthly payments on it.

Renata: That's good. All right, what kind of bed frame should we get?

Nima: I don't really care. The mattress is more important to me.

Renata: Okay! I'll pick out the bed frame. I like the white one.

Nima: Yeah, that one is nice.

Renata: And the price is good.

Nima: Yes.

Renata: Well, that was easy!

Nima: Yes, it was! I was expecting to be shopping for a bed all day!

Renata: Woohoo! Let's go to dinner to celebrate!

Nima: We just spent a lot of money. Maybe we should eat at home.

Renata: Yeah, you're right. Okay, dinner at home it is!

38

아침 일상

-

MORNING ROUTINE (A2)

에밀리아: 매일 몇 시에 일어나세요?

잭: 주 중에는 아침 여섯 시 십오 분쯤 일어나요. 주말에는 아침 일곱 시 반이나 여덟 시쯤 일어나고요. 에밀리아 씨는요?

에밀리아: 월요일부터 금요일까지는 아침 여섯 시 반에 일어나요. 주말에는 아침 여덟 시 쯤 일어나고요. 잭 씨는 일어나면 보통 뭐 하세요?

잭: 샤워를 하고 나서 이 닦고 면도를 해요.

에밀리아: 아 진짜요? 저는 이를 먼저 닦아요. 그러고 나서 샤워를 해요.

잭: 샤워하고 나서 무엇을 해요?

에밀리아: 머리를 말리고 화장을 해요. 면도하고 나서 뭐해요?

잭: 옷을 입고 아침을 먹어요.

에밀리아: 뭐 입고 출근하세요?

잭: 주로 바지와 단추 달린 셔츠를 입어요. 정장은 한 달에 한 번 입고요.

에밀리아: 오, 운이 좋으시네요. 저는 매일 정장을 입고 출근해야 해요!

잭: 정말요? 무슨 일을 하시는 데요?

에밀리아: 저는 변호사예요.

잭: 아, 그렇군요. 매일 아침 준비하는 데 시간이 오래 걸리나요?

에밀리아: 한 시간 반 정도 걸려요. 저는 준비할 때 너무 서두르는 걸 좋아하지 않거든요.

잭: 매일 아침을 드세요?

에밀리아: 그러려고 노력해요! 일을 하려면 에너지가 필요하거든요!

잭: 맞아요, 아침 먹는 것은 중요해요! 가끔 아침을 먹지 않으면, 그만큼 에너지도 없더라고요.

에밀리아: 맞아요. 아침은 하루 중 가장 중요한 식사예요!

잭: 맞아요!

MORNING ROUTINE

Emilia: What time do you wake up every day?

Jack: On weekdays, I wake up around 6:15 a.m. On weekends, I wake up around 7:30 a.m. or 8 a.m. What about you?

Emilia: I wake up at 6:30 a.m. Monday through Friday. On weekends, I get up around 8 a.m. What do you do after you wake up?

Jack: I take a shower and then I brush my teeth and shave.

Emilia: Oh really? I brush my teeth first. And then I take a shower.

Jack: What do you do after you take a shower?

Emilia: I dry my hair and then I put on makeup. What do you do after you shave?

Jack: I get dressed and I eat breakfast.

Emilia: What do you wear to work?

Jack: Usually I wear trousers and a button-down shirt. I wear a suit about once a month.

Emilia: Oh, you're lucky. I have to dress up for work every day!

Jack: Really? What do you do?

Emilia: I'm a lawyer.

Jack: Oh, I see. Does it take you a long time to get ready every morning?

Emilia: It takes me around an hour and a half. I don't like to hurry too much when I'm getting ready.

Jack: Do you eat breakfast every day?

Emilia: I try to! I need energy for work!

Jack: Yeah, it's important to eat breakfast! Sometimes I don't and I don't have as much energy.

Emilia: Yep. Breakfast is the most important meal of the day!

Jack: Exactly!

39

생일 선물

-

BIRTHDAY GIFT (A2)

가비: 마이크한테 줄 선물을 사야해.

숀: 알아. 어떤 걸 사야 좋을까?

가비: 몰라. 마이크는 없는 게 없어.

숀: 흠...

가비: 옷을 사줄까?

숀: 어떤 옷?

가비: 아마도, 셔츠?

숀: 셔츠는 작년에 우리가 사줬었어.

가비: 네 말이 맞아. 선글라스는 어때? 마이크가 선글라스를 엄청 좋아하잖아.

숀: 선글라스는 조금 비싸. 그리고 선글라스가 마이크한테 안 어울릴 수도 있어.

가비: 알았어.

숀: 가게 기프트 카드는 어때?

가비: 기프트 카드는 너무 정이 없어.

숀: 맞아, 하지만 사람들은 기프트 카드 좋아해. 왜냐하면 네가 원하는 걸 살 수 있거든.

가비: 표를 사줄까? 축구 경기나 콘서트 같은?

숀: 오, 그거 좋은 생각이다. 마이크가 스포츠랑 음악을 좋아해.

가비: 이것 봐! 그가 좋아하는 밴드 중 하나가 다음 달에 시내로 온대.

숀: 진짜? 표를 살까?

가비: 응, 그러자!

숀: 만약에 마이크가 쇼에 갈 수 없으면 어쩌지?

가비: 그럼 우리가 가면 돼!

BIRTHDAY GIFT

Gabby: We need to buy a gift for Mike.

Sean: I know. What should we get?

Gabby: I don't know. He has everything.

Sean: Hmm...

Gabby: Should we buy him clothes?

Sean: What kind of clothes?

Gabby: A shirt, maybe?

Sean: We got him a shirt last year.

Gabby: You're right. What about sunglasses? He loves sunglasses.

Sean: Sunglasses are kind of expensive. And maybe they won't look good on him.

Gabby: Okay.

Sean: What about a gift card to a store?

Gabby: Gift cards are so impersonal.

Sean: Yeah, but people like them. Because you can buy whatever you want.

Gabby: Maybe we buy him tickets for something? Like a soccer game or a concert?

Sean: Oh, that's good idea. He likes sports and music.

Gabby: Look at this! One of his favorite bands will be in town next month.

Sean: Really? Should we buy tickets?

Gabby: Yes, let's do it!

Sean: What if he can't go to the show?

Gabby: Then we will go!

40

에이 받았어

-

I GOT AN A (A2)

아이린: 브래드, 나 있잖아.

브래드: 응?

아이린: 나 시험에서 에이 받았어!

브래드: 오, 잘됐다! 역사 시험에서?

아이린: 응. 다섯 시간 공부했어.

브래드: 와. 잘됐다. 나 작년에 그 수업 들었는데 엄청나게 어려웠어.

아이린: 시몬스 선생님이셨어?

브래드: 응.

아이린: 그 교수님는 매우 엄격하셔.

브래드: 맞아. 수업에 있는 모든 사람이 그 교수님을 매우 무서워했어! 하지만 우리는 많이 배웠어.

아이린: 응, 나는 엄청나게 많이 배우고 있어. 사실 교수님 수업을 듣기 전에는 역사를 좋아하지 않았는데, 지금은 역사에 매우 관심이 많아.

브래드: 진짜?

아이린: 응.

브래드: 그래서 넌 어떻게 공부했어? 노트를 다시 읽은 것뿐이야?

아이린: 응.

브래드: 나도 그렇게 교수님 수업 시험을 공부했는데 에이를 받은 적이 한번도 없어!

아이린: 음, 나는 오랫동안 공부했어! 그리고 이번 수업 내용을 정말 좋아했어. 그게 좋은 점수를 받는 데 도움이 된 것 같아.

브래드: 말이 되네. 내가 좋아하는 수업에서 항상 점수를 잘 받아.

아이린: 나도. 수학에서 더 좋은 점수를 받았으면 좋겠지만 나는 수학이 너무 싫어.

브래드: 나는 수학을 정말 좋아해! 내가 너한테 수학을 도와주고, 네가 나한테 역사를 도와주면 되겠어.

아이린: 좋아, 콜!

I GOT AN A

Irene: Guess what, Brad?

Brad: What?

Irene: I got an A on my test!

Brad: Oh, that's great! On your history test?

Irene: Yeah. I studied for five hours.

Brad: Wow. Good for you. I took that class last year and it was so hard.

Irene: Did you have Ms. Simmons?

Brad: Yeah.

Irene: She's really strict.

Brad: Yes, she is. Everyone in the class was so scared of her! But we learned a lot.

Irene: Yeah, I'm learning so much. Actually, I didn't like history before I took her class, but now I'm really interested in it.

Brad: Really?

Irene: Mmm hmm.

Brad: So how did you study? Did you just read your notes again?

Irene: Yep.

Brad: That's how I studied for tests in her class too, but I never got As!

Irene: Well, I studied for a long time! But I also loved this chapter. So, I think that helped me get a good grade.

Brad: That makes sense. I always get better grades in the classes that I like.

Irene: Me too. I wish I got better grades in math, but I hate math.

Brad: And I love math! Maybe I can help you with math and you can help me with history.

Irene: Okay, deal!

41

그는 좋은 운전자야

-

HE'S A GOOD DRIVER (A2)

존: 잭슨이 걱정돼.

에이다: 왜?

존: 잭슨이 곧 운전 면허증을 딸 거야!

에이다: 응, 그거 조금 무섭네. 근데 그게 우리한테는 좋은 걸! 더는 잭슨을 여기저기 태워 주지 않아도 되잖아.

존: 맞아. 하지만 이 도시에는 정상이 아닌 운전자들이 너무 많아.

에이다: 알아. 하지만 잭슨은 운전을 잘 해!

존: 응, 내가 가르쳐 줬기 때문이지.

에이다: 그것도 한 가지 이유네. 하지만 걔가 책임감이 있는 청년이기도 해.

존: 응, 맞아. 우리는 운이 좋은 부모야.

에이다: 응, 맞아. 운전 면허 시험이 언제지? 다음 달이지, 맞지?

존: 이번 달 말에 필기시험을 보고 십오 일에 실기시험이 있어.

에이다: 정말 금방이네. 하지만 잭슨은 준비가 됐어.

존: 거의. 나는 같이 좀 더 연습했으면 좋겠어. 주차를 더 잘해야 해.

에이다: 내가 걔한테 주차하는 방법을 가르쳐야겠어. 우리 가족 중에서 주차 장인은 나잖아.

존: 맞아. 당신의 기술은 누구와도 비교할 수 없지.

에이다: 고마워! 그럼, 잭슨이랑 다음 운전 수업은 언제야?

존: 축구 경기가 끝난 토요일 오후야.

에이다: 알았어. 잘 됐으면 좋겠다!

HE'S A GOOD DRIVER

John: I'm worried about Jackson.

Ada: Why?

John: He's getting his driver's license soon!

Ada: Yeah, that's a little scary. But that's good for us! We won't have to drive him everywhere anymore.

John: True. But there are so many crazy drivers in this city.

Ada: I know. But he's a good driver!

John: Yes, because I taught him how to drive.

Ada: That's one reason why. But he's also a responsible young man.

John: Yeah, he is. We're lucky parents.

Ada: Yes, we are. When is his driving test? It's next month, right?

John: He has his written test at the end of this month and his behind-the-wheel test on the fifteenth.

Ada: That's really soon. But he's ready.

John: Almost. I still want to practice some more with him. He needs to get better at parking.

Ada: I should teach him how to park. I'm the best parker in this family.

John: That's true. Your skills are unmatched.

Ada: Thanks! So, when is your next driving lesson with Jackson?

John: Saturday afternoon after his soccer game.

Ada: Okay. I hope it goes well!

42

저건 귀신이야?

-

IS THAT A GHOST? (A2)

테일러: 저거 뭐야?!

스펜서: 뭐가 뭐야?

테일러: 구석에 있는 저거?

스펜서: 뭔데? 아무것도 안 보여.

테일러: 그것처럼 보여... 아니다... 그럴리가.

스펜서: 뭐?! 너 때문에 무섭잖아!

테일러: 귀신같이 보여!

스펜서: 아, 그만해. 귀신 안 믿어.

테일러: 나도 안 믿어. 그런데 귀신처럼 생겼어.

스펜서: 그게 어떻게 생겼는데?

테일러: 사람의 형태였는데 그 몸이 투명해서 뒤가 비치더라고.

스펜서: 널 믿지 않아. 네가 나한테 장난치는 것 같아.

테일러: 장난 아니야! 그게 내가 본 거라고!

스펜서: 네가 아마 그냥 상상한 것일 거야.

테일러: 그렇게 생각 안해.

스펜서: ...

테일러: 뭐?

스펜서: ...세상에.

테일러: 뭐?!

스펜서: 저거 보여?

테일러: 그래! 저게 내가 아까 본거야!

스펜서: 귀신처럼 보여!

테일러: 내가 말했잖아!

스펜서: 알았어. 이젠 널 믿을 것 같아.

테일러: 고마워! 이제 난 갈래.

스펜서: 어디 가?

테일러: 귀신이 여기 있잖아! 여기를 떠날 거야!

스펜서: 귀신과 함께 나를 혼자 두고 가면 안되지!

테일러: 그럼, 같이 가!

스펜서: 알았어. 안녕, 귀신! 제발 떠나서 다시는 돌아오지 마!

IS THAT A GHOST?

Taylor: What is that?!

Spencer: What is *what*?

Taylor: That thing in the corner?

Spencer: What thing? I don't see anything.

Taylor: It looks like... no... that's not possible.

Spencer: What?! You're scaring me!

Taylor: It looked like a ghost!

Spencer: Oh, stop. I don't believe in ghosts.

Taylor: I don't either. But that looked like a ghost.

Spencer: What did it look like?

Taylor: It was in the shape of a person, and I could see through it.

Spencer: I don't believe you. I think you're playing a joke on me.

Taylor: I'm not joking! That's what I saw!

Spencer: You probably just imagined it.

Taylor: I don't think so.

Spencer: ...

Taylor: What?

Spencer: ...oh my gosh.

Taylor: What?!

Spencer: Do you see that?

Taylor: YES! That's what I saw before!

Spencer: That looks like a ghost!

Taylor: I told you!

Spencer: Okay. Maybe I believe you now.

Taylor: Thank you! Now I'm leaving.

Spencer: Where are you going?

Taylor: There is a ghost in here! I'm getting out of here!

Spencer: You can't leave me here alone with a ghost!

Taylor: So, come with me!

Spencer: Okay. Bye, ghost! Please leave and don't come back!

43

귀여운 개
-
CUTE DOG (A2)

제니: 실례합니다. 그 쪽 개한테 인사해도 될까요?

줄리안: 물론이죠! 매우 좋아할 거예요.

제니: 너무 귀여워요! 어떤 종류의 개예요?

줄리안: 잘 모르겠어요. 구조됐어요.

제니: 치와와 믹스견 같아요.

줄리안: 사실, 스패니얼과 포메라니안이 조금씩 섞여 있다고 생각해요.

제니: 그렇군요.

줄리안: 아주 작은 골든 리트리버처럼 보이는 것 같아요.

제니: 저도 그렇게 생각해요! 강아지인가요?

줄리안: 아니요, 사실 여섯 살이예요.

제니: 우와! 하지만 강아지처럼 생겼어요!

줄리안: 네, 영원히 강아지처럼 보일 것 같아요.

제니: 그러길 바래요. 매우 부드러워요! 부드러운 털이 참 좋네요.

줄리안: 네 정말로 털이 부드러워요. 건강한 사료를 먹는 데 그게 털이 부드럽도록 도와줘요.

제니: 정말 친절하시네요. 강아지 이름이 뭐예요?

줄리안: 스탠리요.

제니: 개 이름이 재미있네요. 정말 귀여운 것 같아요!

줄리안: 감사합니다.

제니: 어디서 데려 왔어요?

줄리안: 보호소에서요. 스탠리는 구조견이에요.

제니: 굉장해요! 저희 강아지도 마찬가지예요. 사랑스러워요.

줄리안: 멋지네요! 개를 키우신 지 얼마나 되셨어요?

제니: 한 살일 때 데려와서 지금 네 살이니까 삼 년 정도 됐네요.

줄리안: 어떤 종류의 개인가요? 그리고 이름이 뭐예요?

제니: 이름은 코코고 푸들 믹스견이에요.

줄리안: 좋네요.

제니: 스탠리가 코코를 좋아할 것 같아요?

줄리안: 그러길 바래요. 강아지들을 위해 놀이 시간을 정할까요?

제니: 물론이죠! 그렇게 하고 싶어요.

CUTE DOG

Jenny: Excuse me. May I say hello to your dog?

Julian: Sure! He would like that very much.

Jenny: He's so cute! What kind of dog is he?

Julian: I'm not sure. He is a rescue.

Jenny: He looks like a Chihuahua mix.

Julian: Actually, I think he's part spaniel and part Pomeranian.

Jenny: I see.

Julian: I think he actually looks like a very tiny golden retriever.

Jenny: I think so, too! Is he a puppy?

Julian: No, he is actually six years old.

Jenny: Wow! But he looks like a puppy!

Julian: Yeah, I think he will look like a puppy forever.

Jenny: I hope so. He is so soft! I love his soft fur.

Julian: He does have soft fur. He eats healthy dog food and it helps his fur stay silky.

Jenny: That's very nice of you. What's his name?

Julian: Stanley.

Jenny: That's a funny name for a dog. I think it's so cute!

Julian: Thank you.

Jenny: Where did you get him?

Julian: At the shelter. Stanley is a rescue dog.

Jenny: That's awesome! So is mine. She is lovely.

Julian: Cool! How long have you had your dog?

Jenny: I got her when she was one, and now she's four, so about three years.

Julian: What kind of dog is she? And what's her name?

Jenny: Her name is Coco and she's a poodle mix.

Julian: That's nice.

Jenny: Do you think Stanley would like Coco?

Julian: I hope so. Should we schedule a playtime for them?

Jenny: Sure! I would like that.

44

유성우
-
A METEOR SHOWER (A2)

안드레아: 마이클, 있잖아!

마이클: 뭐?

안드레아: 오늘 밤에 유성우가 내릴 거야! 뉴스에서 봤어.

마이클: 아, 진짜? 유성우가 언제 내려?

안드레아: 유성우는 오후 아홉 시에 시작해서 자정 무렵에 끝날 거야.

마이클: 집에서 유성우를 볼 수 있을까?

안드레아: 아니, 집은 도시의 불빛이 너무 많아. 아주 어두운 곳으로 가야 해.

마이클: 펠릭스 산 정상까지 차를 타고 가면 되겠어.

안드레아: 얼마나 멀어?

마이클: 여기서 십 마일 정도 떨어져 있는 것 같아.

안드레아: 그렇게 하자.

마이클: 너 유성우 본 적 있어?

안드레아: 없어. 이번이 처음이 될 거야. 너무 기뻐. 나는 별똥별을 본 적이 없어.

마이클: 네가 기쁘다니 나도 기뻐!

안드레아: 너는 별똥별 본 적 있어?

마이클: 응.

안드레아: 언제?

마이클: 몇 년 전에 유성우가 내렸어. 내가 펠릭스 산에 캠프에서 일하고 있었거든. 그날 밤 별똥별을 엄청 봤어.

안드레아: 소원 빌었어?

마이클: 응, 빌었어.

안드레아: 무슨 소원 빌었어?

마이클: 너한테 말할 수 없어! 말하면 내 소원이 이루어지지 않을 거야.

안드레아: 아직도 이뤄지지 않았다는 말이야?

마이클: 응...

안드레아: 그럼, 오늘 밤에 새로운 소원을 빌 수 있길 바래.

마이클: 그렇기를 바래.

A METEOR SHOWER

Andrea: Michael, guess what!

Michael: What?

Andrea: There's going to be a meteor shower tonight! I saw it on the news.

Michael: Oh, really? What time will the meteor shower happen?

Andrea: The meteor shower will start at 9:00 p.m. and end around midnight.

Michael: Can we watch the meteor shower from home?

Andrea: No, there are too many city lights at home. We have to go somewhere very dark.

Michael: We can drive to the top of Mt. Felix.

Andrea: How far is it?

Michael: I think the mountain is ten miles from here.

Andrea: Let's do that.

Michael: Have you ever seen a meteor shower?

Andrea: I haven't. This will be my first time. I'm very excited. I have never seen a shooting star before.

Michael: I'm very excited for you!

Andrea: Have you seen a shooting star before?

Michael: Yes.

Andrea: When?

Michael: There was a meteor shower a few years ago. I was working at a camp on Mt. Felix. I saw many shooting stars that night.

Andrea: Did you make a wish?

Michael: Yes, I did.

Andrea: What did you wish for?

Michael: I can't tell you! If I tell you, my wish won't come true.

Andrea: You mean it still hasn't come true?

Michael: No...

Andrea: Well, hopefully we can make some new wishes tonight.

Michael: I hope so.

45

좋은 사진 찍는 방법

-

HOW TO TAKE A GOOD PICTURE (A2)

마이아: 안녕, 데미안!

데미안: 안녕, 마이아! 오랜만이야.

마이아: 맞아! 어떻게 지냈어?

데미안: 잘 지냈어. 너는?

마이아: 잘 지냈어. 아, 너한테 물어볼 게 있어. 너 사진작가 맞지?

데미안: 응. 근데, 나는 그냥 재미로 찍어. 나는 전문 사진작가는 아니야.

마이아: 하지만 네 사진은 전문적으로 보여!

데미안: 아, 고마워! 사진 찍는 건 내 취미고 오랫동안 해왔어.

마이아: 사진을 잘 찍을 수 있는 비결이 좀 있어?

데미안: 음... 알았어. 어떤 사진 찍는 걸 좋아해?

마이아: 대부분 풍경과 건축물이야.

데미안: 아, 알았어. "삼등분 법칙"에 대해 들어본 적 있어?

마이아: 아니. 그게 뭐야?

데미안: 자, 직사각형을 생각해봐. 그러고 나서 직사각형을 아홉 개의 똑같은 정사각형으로 나눠. 사진에서 가장 중요한 부분은 수직선과 수평선이 만나는 곳에 있어야 해. 이게 네 사진 구성에 도움이 될 거야.

마이아: 오, 정말? 멋지다! 그렇게 해볼게.

데미안: 응, 해봐. 난 가봐야 해. 나중에 팁이 더 필요하면 말해!

마이아: 그럴게. 고마워, 데미안!

데미안: 천만에. 나중에 보자.

마이아: 안녕!

HOW TO TAKE A GOOD PICTURE

Maia: Hey, Damien!

Damien: Hi, Maia! Long time no see.

Maia: I know! How have you been?

Damien: Pretty good. How about you?

Maia: I'm good. Oh, I have a question for you. You're a photographer, right?

Damien: Yeah. Well, I take pictures just for fun. I'm not a professional photographer.

Maia: But your pictures look professional!

Damien: Oh, thanks! It's my hobby, and I have been doing it for a long time.

Maia: Do you have any tips on how to take good pictures?

Damien: Umm... sure. What do you like to take pictures of?

Maia: Mostly landscapes and architecture.

Damien: Ah, okay. Have you heard of the "Rule of Thirds"?

Maia: No. What's that?

Damien: So, imagine a rectangle. And then divide the rectangle into nine equal squares. The most important parts of the photo should be at the places where the vertical and horizontal lines meet. This will help the composition of your photo.

Maia: Oh, really? That's so cool! I'll try that.

Damien: Yeah, you should. Well, I have to go. If you need any more tips in the future, let me know!

Maia: I will. Thanks, Damien!

Damien: No problem. See you later.

Maia: See you!

46

깜짝 파티
-
A SURPRISE PARTY (A2)

인그리드: 야, 너 엠마 깜짝 파티에 올 거야?

에릭: 쉿! 그렇게 크게 얘기하지 마. 엠마가 들으면 어쩌려고.

인그리드: 엠마는 옆방에서 댄이랑 이야기하고 있어. 내 말 못 들어.

에릭: 네가 말을 할 때는 모든 사람이 들을 수 있어.

인그리드: 모든 사람은 아니야. 다른 도시의 사람들은 내 말 못 듣지.

에릭: 확실해?

인그리드: 알았어, 알았어, 나 시끄러워. 알겠어. 그래서, 너는 올 거야?

에릭: 응. 너는?

인그리드: 물론이지, 계획 세우는 걸 도와주고 있어.

에릭: 그래서, 계획이 뭔데?

인그리드: 엠마의 남자친구인 아론이 엠마를 저녁 식사에 데려갈 거야. 다른 사람들은 전부 여섯 시에서 여섯 시 반 사이에 집에 도착하고. 엠마와 아론은 여덟 시까지 집에 돌아와야 해. 아론이 메시지로 우리에게 계속해서 상황을 알려 줄거야. 우리는 모두 숨어 있다가, 얘네가 집에 오면 뛰쳐나와 "놀랐지!"라고 외치는 거지.

에릭: 좋아. 엠마는 전혀 의심하고 있지 않아? 자기 생일에 아무도 같이 놀고 싶어 하지 않는데, 거기에 대해 놀라고 있지 않아?

인그리드: 걔 생일 지나고 이번 주말에 친구들이랑 놀 거야. 그게 유일한 파티라고 생각하고 있고.

에릭: 그래서 엠마는 깜짝 파티에 대해 전혀 모르고 있어?

인그리드: 어! 완전 아무것도 모르고 있어.

에릭: 멋지네. 엠마의 반응을 빨리 보고 싶어.

인그리드: 나도!

A SURPRISE PARTY

Ingrid: Hey, are you coming to Emma's surprise party?

Erik: Shh! Don't say that so loud. She might hear you.

Ingrid: She's in the next room talking to Dan. She can't hear me.

Erik: Everyone can hear you when you talk.

Ingrid: Not *everyone*. People in other cities can't hear me.

Erik: Are you sure?

Ingrid: Okay, okay, I'm loud. I get it. Anyway, are you coming?

Erik: Yeah. Are you?

Ingrid: Of course, I'm helping plan it.

Erik: So, what's the plan?

Ingrid: Her boyfriend Aaron is taking her out to dinner. Everyone is arriving at the house between six and six thirty. Emma and Aaron should get back to the house by eight. Aaron is going to keep us updated via text. We're all going to hide, and then when they come home, we'll jump out and say "Surprise!"

Erik: Cool. Is she suspicious at all? Isn't she surprised that none of her friends want to hang out for her birthday?

Ingrid: She's hanging out with her friends this weekend, after her birthday. So, she thinks that's the only party.

Erik: And she has no idea about the surprise party?

Ingrid: Nope! She's totally clueless.

Erik: Awesome. I can't wait to see her reaction.

Ingrid: Me too!

47

내가 좋아하는 아침

-

MY FAVORITE BREAKFAST (A2)

케이토: 오늘 아침으로 뭐 먹을래?

한나: 음... 과일과 요구르트 아니면 시리얼. 시리얼이 좋은데 그게 그다지 건강하지 않다는 걸 알아. 그래서 과일, 요구르트, 그레놀라를 먹으려고 해.

케이토: 아, 알겠어. 오트밀 먹어 봤어? 오트밀은 정말 건강에 좋잖아, 맞지?

한나: 응, 맞아. 하지만 너무 시시해! 너는 아침으로 뭘 먹을 거야?

케이토: 된장국과 쌀밥을 먹으려고.

한나: 우와! 여기 미국에서는 점심이나 저녁에만 그런 음식을 먹어.

케이토: 응, 우리도 된장국과 밥은 점심이나 저녁에 먹어. 나는 아침으로 먹는 걸 좋아하고. 정말 배가 고프고, 요리할 시간이 있을 때는 가끔 된장국과 밥, 그리고 생선구이를 먹기도 해.

한나: 흥미롭다! 나는 아침으로 생선을 먹어본 적이 없어.

케이토: 언젠가 한 번 해봐! 건강에 좋아.

한나: 건강에 좋아 보여. 해 봐야겠어!

케이토: 가끔 나도 아침에 시리얼을 먹어. 하지만 시리얼 먹기 가장 좋은 시간은 늦은 저녁에 야식으로 먹는 거야.

한나: 나도! 하루 중 언제라도 시리얼은 좋아.

케이토: 하하. 알았어, 오늘은 된장국과 밥을 먹고, 내일은 시리얼을 먹는 게 어때?

한나: 좋아!

MY FAVORITE BREAKFAST

Keito: What do you want for breakfast today?

Hannah: Hmm... fruit and yogurt or cereal. I love cereal but I know it's not super healthy for me. So, I'm trying to eat fruit and yogurt and granola.

Keito: Oh, I see. Have you tried oatmeal? Oatmeal is really healthy, right?

Hannah: Yes, it is, but it's so boring! What are you going to eat for breakfast?

Keito: Probably some miso soup and steamed rice.

Hannah: Oh, wow! Here in the U.S. we only eat that kind of thing for lunch or dinner.

Keito: Yeah, we also eat miso soup and rice for lunch and/or dinner. I like to eat it for breakfast. Sometimes I eat grilled fish with my miso soup and rice if I'm really hungry and I have time to make it.

Hannah: Interesting! I've never had fish for breakfast.

Keito: You should try it sometime! It's healthy.

Hannah: That does sound healthy. Maybe I will!

Keito: I eat cereal for breakfast sometimes too. But my favorite time to eat cereal is as a late-night snack.

Hannah: Me too! Any time of day is good for cereal.

Keito: Ha ha. Okay, how about we have some miso soup and rice today, and tomorrow we can have cereal?

Hannah: Sounds good!

48

짜증나는 이웃

-

MY ANNOYING NEIGHBORS (A2)

나디아: 우리 이웃이 또 음악을 시끄럽게 틀고 있어!

카덱: 아. 그 사람이 음악 소리 좀 낮추겠다고 한 것 같은데!

나디아: 마음을 바꿨나 봐. 우리가 여기에 대해 세 번이나 얘기했어. 너무 예의가 없어!

카덱: 어떻게 하지?

나디아: 우리 집주인과 얘기를 해야 할까?

카덱: 흠... 우리가 그 사람한테 한 번 더 얘기하고 그 다음에 집주인과 얘기 하는 게 어때?

나디아: 뭐라고? 음악 때문에 안들려!

카덱: 우리가 그 사람에게 한 번 더 얘기하고 그 다음에 집주인과 얘기 하는 것이 어떠냐고. 어떻게 생각해?

나디아: 좋은 생각인 것 같아. 오, 소리를 줄였어.

카덱: 우리가 소리 지르는 걸 들었나 봐.

나디아: 아마도.

카덱: 이래서 내가 더 조용한 동네로 이사가고 싶다니까.

나디아: 응. 하지만 이 도시에 조용한 동네들은 더 비싸.

카덱: 전부다 그런 건 아니야. 댄이랑 신디는 크레스트뷰에 사는데, 거긴 꽤 조용하면서 저렴해.

나디아: 맞아. 온라인으로 살펴보고 구할 수 있는 아파트가 있는지 봐야겠어.

카덱: 뭐라고? 안 들려.

나디아: 온라인을 살펴보고 구할 수 있는 아파트가 있는지 봐야겠어.

카덱: 알았어. 지금 하자. 우리가 여기에 더 오래 있다가는 목소리가 나가버릴거야!

ANNOYING NEIGHBORS

Nadia: Our neighbor is playing loud music again!

Kadek: Ugh. I thought he said he would keep the music down!

Nadia: I guess he changed his mind. We've talked to him about it three times. It's so rude!

Kadek: What can we do?

Nadia: Should we talk to our landlord?

Kadek: Hmm... maybe we should talk to him one more time and then talk to the landlord?

Nadia: What? I can't hear you over the music!

Kadek: I SAID WE SHOULD TALK TO HIM ONE MORE TIME AND THEN TALK TO THE LANDLORD. WHAT DO YOU THINK?

Nadia: I THINK THAT'S A GOOD IDEA. Oh, he turned it down.

Kadek: Maybe he heard us shouting.

Nadia: Possibly.

Kadek: This is why I want to move to a quieter neighborhood.

Nadia: Yeah. But all the quieter neighborhoods in this city are more expensive.

Kadek: Not all of them. Dan and Cindy live in Crestview, which is pretty quiet and affordable.

Nadia: That's true. Maybe we should look online and see if there are any available apartments.

Kadek: What? I can't hear you.

Nadia: MAYBE WE SHOULD LOOK ONLINE AND SEE IF THERE ARE ANY APARTMENTS FOR RENT.

Kadek: Okay. Let's do it now. We're going to lose our voices if we stay here much longer!

49

미용실에서 일어난 잘못된 의사소통

-

MISCOMMUNICATION AT THE SALON (A2)

브리아나: 안녕하세요, 도미닉 씨! 만나서 반가워요! 들어와서 앉으세요.

도미닉: 감사합니다, 브리아나.

브리아나: 우와, 머리가 길었네요! 머리 자를 준비 되셨나요?

도미닉: 물론이죠! 내일 면접 볼 때 멋져 보여야 해요.

브리아나: 제가 도와 드릴 수 있어요. 오늘 어떤 걸 해드릴까요?

도미닉: 윗부분은 길게 하고 옆쪽은 매우 짧게 하고 싶어요.

브리아나: 위쪽도 잘라드릴까요?

도미닉: 네, 위에는 일 인치 잘라주세요.

브리아나: 알겠어요. 다른 건 어떻게 되어가고 있어요?

도미닉: 잘 되어 가고 있어요. 내일 면접만 잘 보도록 확실히 하면 돼요.

브리아나: 도미닉 씨가 면접을 틀림없이 잘 볼 거라고 확신해요.

도미닉: 그러길 바래요.

브리아나: 여자친구는 잘 지내나요?

도미닉: 잘지내요. 다음 주에 같이 여행 갈 거예요.

브리아나: 어디로 가세요?

도미닉: 함께 발리로 갈거예요.

브리아나: 재밌겠네요! 발리는 아름답다고 들었어요.

도미닉: 네, 너무 신나요!

브리아나: 여행은 얼마나 가나요?

도미닉: 이 주 정도 가요.

브리아나: 좋네요!

도미닉: 감사해요! 전 사실—이런! 뭐하시는 거예요?

브리아나: 네? 제가 뭘 잘못했나요?

도미닉: 머리를 너무 많이 잘랐어요!

브리아나: 무슨 말이에요? 머리 일 인치만 남겨 두라고 하셨잖아요, 맞죠?

도미닉: 아니요, 일 인치 잘라 달라고 했죠!

브리아나: 오... 죄송합니다. 이번에 머리 자른 건 값을 받지 않겠습니다. 머리는 저희가 고쳐드릴 수 있어요!

MISCOMMUNICATION AT THE SALON

Briana: Hi, Dominic! Good to see you! Come in and have a seat.

Dominic: Thanks, Briana.

Briana: Wow, your hair is getting long! Are you ready for your haircut?

Dominic: I sure am! I need to look good for my interview tomorrow.

Briana: I can help with that. What would you like me to do today?

Dominic: I want to keep the top long and the sides very short.

Briana: Do you want me to cut the top?

Dominic: Yes, let's cut an inch off the top.

Briana: Gotcha. How is everything else going?

Dominic: Everything else is going okay. I just need to make sure my interview goes well tomorrow.

Briana: I'm sure you will do well on your interview.

Dominic: I hope so.

Briana: How is your girlfriend doing?

Dominic: She is good. We're going on a trip together next week.

Briana: Where are you going?

Dominic: We're going to Bali together.

Briana: That sounds exciting! I heard Bali is beautiful.

Dominic: Yes, I am very excited!

Briana: How long is your trip?

Dominic: We are going for about two weeks.

Briana: I'm happy for you!

Dominic: Thanks! I actually—hey! What are you doing?

Briana: Huh? Did I do something wrong?

Dominic: You cut off so much hair!

Briana: What do you mean? You said leave an inch of hair, right?

Dominic: No, I said cut off an inch!

Briana: Oh... I'm so sorry. I won't charge you for this cut. We can fix this!

50

열쇠를 차 안에 두고 잠갔어

-

I LOCKED MY KEYS IN THE CAR (A2)

아자드: 아, 안돼.

브렌나: 왜?

아자드: 나 방금 멍청한 짓을 했어.

브렌나: 뭘 했는데?

아자드: 열쇠를 차 안에 두고 잠갔어.

브렌나: 오, 이런. 어쩌다 그랬어?

아자드: 차에서 가방을 전부 꺼내려고 했어. 그러다가 깜빡하고 열쇠를 자리에 놓았지 뭐야.

브렌나: 어떻게 하지?

아자드: 자물쇠 수리공을 불러야 해.

브렌나: 자물쇠 수리공은 너무 비싸! 지난번에 차 안에 열쇠를 두고 잠갔는데 백 달러를 내야 했어. 차를 여는 데 오 분밖에 걸리지 않았는데 말이야!

아자드: 알아. 너무 바가지야. 하지만 어떻게 열쇠를 꺼내야 할지 모르겠어.

브렌나: 창문을 조금 열어 볼래?

아자드: 해볼게.

(오 분 후...)

아자드: 못하겠어! 자물쇠 수리공을 불러야 겠어.

브렌나: 알았어. 내가 온라인으로 봤는데 저렴한 곳 하나 찾았어. 이 수리공은 칠십오 달러밖에 받지 않아.

아자드: 그게 싸다고?

브렌나: 아니지. 하지만 백 달러보다는 낫잖아!

아자드: 응, 그런 것 같네.

브렌나: 그가 사십오 분 안에 여기로 온다고 했어.

아자드: 사십오 분?!

브렌나: 그게 그 수리공이 여기로 가장 빨리 올 수 있는 시간이야! 차 안에 열쇠를 두고 잠근 건 네 잘못이지.

아자드: 네 말이 맞아. 지금부터 열쇠를 조심히 다룰거야.

I LOCKED MY KEYS IN THE CAR

Azad: Oh, no.

Brenna: What?

Azad: I just did something stupid.

Brenna: What did you do?

Azad: I locked my keys in the car.

Brenna: Oh, dear. How did that happen?

Azad: I was trying to take all of these bags out of the car. Then I got distracted and left my keys on the seat.

Brenna: What should we do?

Azad: I think we need to call a locksmith.

Brenna: Locksmiths are so expensive! The last time I locked my keys in the car I had to pay one hundred dollars. And it only took him five minutes to open the car!

Azad: I know. It's a rip-off. But I don't know how to get the keys out.

Brenna: Can you try to open the window a little?

Azad: I'll try.

(Five minutes later...)

Azad: I can't do it! I have to call the locksmith.

Brenna: Okay. I looked online and found a cheap one. He only charges seventy-five dollars.

Azad: That's cheap?

Brenna: Well, no. But it's better than one hundred dollars!

Azad: Yeah, I guess.

Brenna: He said he'll be here in forty-five minutes.

Azad: Forty-five minutes?!

Brenna: That's the fastest he can get here! It's your fault for locking the keys in the car.

Azad: You're right. From now on I'm going to be so careful with my keys!

51

양 세기

-

COUNTING SHEEP (A2)

울리히: 안녕, 일라이자.
일라이자: 안녕, 울리히. 어떻게 지내?
울리히: 괜찮게 지내.
일라이자: 확실해? 별로 안 좋아 보여.
울리히: 지난밤에 두 시간 밖에 못 잤어.
일라이자: 오, 이런!
울리히: 너무 피곤해.
일라이자: 어젯밤에 무슨 일이 있었어?
울리히: 잘 모르겠어. 그냥 잠이 안오더라고.
일라이자: 이상하다.
울리히: 그렇지. 뭘 해야 할지 모르겠어.
일라이자: 잠자기 전에 우유 마셔 봤어?
울리히: 아니, 난 우유를 안좋아해.
일라이자: 그렇구나.
울리히: 열 살 때부터 우유를 안마셨어.
일라이자: 오래전이네.
울리히: 응. 또 다른 방법 있어?
일라이자: 양을 세어 봤어?
울리히: 나는 양이 없는 걸.
일라이자: 아니, 내 말은 상상 속의 양을 세라는 거야.
울리히: 그게 효과가 있어?

일라이자: 많은 사람에게 효과가 있다고 들었어.

울리히: 알았어, 그래서 어떻게 해?

일라이자: 첫째로, 울타리를 뛰어넘는 한 마리 양을 상상해봐. 그게 너의 첫 번째 양이 될 거야.

울리히: 그러고 나서?

일라이자: 둘째로, 울타리를 뛰어넘는 또 다른 양을 상상해봐. 그게 너의 두 번째 양이 될 거야.

울리히: 알았어.

일라이자: 잠이 들 때까지 양을 세는거야. 해봐!

울리히: 하나, 둘, 셋, 넷... 다섯... 여....

일라이자: 아... 울리히?

울리히: Zzzzz.

일라이자: 잠들었네. 되게 피곤했나 보네.

COUNTING SHEEP

Ulrich: Hi, Eliza.

Eliza: Hi, Ulrich. How are you?

Ulrich: I'm okay.

Eliza: Are you sure? You don't look well.

Ulrich: I only slept two hours last night.

Eliza: Oh, no!

Ulrich: I am so tired.

Eliza: What happened last night?

Ulrich: I'm not sure. I just couldn't fall asleep.

Eliza: That's strange.

Ulrich: I know. I don't know what to do.

Eliza: Have you tried drinking milk before you go to bed?

Ulrich: No, I don't like milk.

Eliza: I understand.

Ulrich: I stopped drinking milk when I was ten.

Eliza: That was a long time ago.

Ulrich: It was. Do you have another idea?

Eliza: Have you tried counting sheep?

Ulrich: I don't own any sheep.

Eliza: No, I mean counting imaginary sheep.

Ulrich: Does that work?

Eliza: I heard it works for many people.

Ulrich: Okay, so what do I do?

Eliza: First, imagine one sheep jumping over a fence. That will be your first sheep.

Ulrich: And then what?

Eliza: Second, imagine another sheep jumping over a fence. That will be your second sheep.

Ulrich: Okay.

Eliza: You count these sheep until you fall asleep. Try it!

Ulrich: One, two, three, four… five… si….

Eliza: Uh… Ulrich?

Ulrich: Zzzzz.

Eliza: He fell asleep. I guess he was very tired.

52

대학 첫날
-
FIRST DAY AT COLLEGE (A2)

엄마: 중요한 날 앞두고 준비는 다 됐어?

트레버: 네. 엄마랑 아빠도 괜찮겠어요?

엄마: 우리는 괜찮을 거야. 네가 보고 싶을 거야.

트레버: 엄마, 학교는 고작 두 시간 거리에 있어요.

엄마: 그래도 우리는 여전히 네가 보고 싶을 거야.

트레버: 알았어요.

엄마: 신나니?

트레버: 네. 약간 긴장되기도 해요.

엄마: 괜찮아! 너는 잘 지낼 거야.

트레버: 그러길 바래요.

엄마: 존은 언제 여기로 오니?

트레버: 모르겠어요.

엄마: 존이 너와 같이 학교에 가서 기뻐.

트레버: 저도요. 존은 훌륭한 룸메이트가 될 거예요.

엄마: 수업들을 준비는 됐니?

트레버: 아니요, 하지만 수업은 다음 주부터 시작해요. 시간 많아요.

엄마: 네 물건을 옮길 때 도움이 필요하니?

트레버: 아니요, 다른 학생들이 도와줄 거 같아요.

엄마: 확실해?

트레버: 네, 엄마. 집에 가도 돼요. 저는 괜찮을 거예요.

엄마: 점심 같이 먹을래?

트레버: 아니요, 오늘 점심은 무료예요. 학생들 전부 거기에 있을 거고요.

엄마: 알았어...

트레버: 엄마, 저는 괜찮을 거예요.

엄마: 네가 그렇다면.

트레버: 사랑해요. 아빠한테도 저 괜찮을 거라고 말해 주세요.

엄마: 나도 사랑해. 즐거운 시간 보내!

FIRST DAY AT COLLEGE

Mom: Are you ready for your big day?

Trevor: Yep. Are you and Dad going to be okay?

Mom: I think we will be okay. We are going to miss you.

Trevor: Mom, school is only two hours away.

Mom: We will still miss you.

Trevor: All right.

Mom: Are you excited?

Trevor: Yeah. I'm also a little nervous.

Mom: That's okay! You will have lots of fun.

Trevor: I hope so.

Mom: When will John be here?

Trevor: I don't know.

Mom: I'm glad he is going to school with you.

Trevor: Me too. John is going to be a great roommate.

Mom: Are you ready for class?

Trevor: No, but classes start next week. I have lots of time.

Mom: Do you need help with your things?

Trevor: No, I think other students will help.

Mom: Are you sure?

Trevor: Yes, Mom. You can go home. I will be fine.

Mom: Do you want to get lunch together?

Trevor: No, lunch is free today. All of the other students will be there.

Mom: Okay...

Trevor: Mom, I will be fine.

Mom: If you say so.

Trevor: I love you. Tell Dad I will be fine.

Mom: I love you, too. Have a great time!

53

동물원에서 탈출한 동물

-

ESCAPED ANIMAL AT THE ZOO (A2)

티나: 안녕하세요, 제프 씨! 오늘 기분이 어떠세요?

제프: 좋아요. 그런데 토니 본 적 있어요?

티나: 토니가 누구예요? 어떻게 생겼어요?

제프: 토니는 여기에 살아요. 그는 주황색과 흰색 바탕에 검은색 줄무늬를 갖고 있고 오백 파운드 정도의 무게가 나가요.

티나: 꽤 무겁네요! 잠시만요... 주황색과 흰색 바탕에 검은색 줄무늬요?

제프: 네.

티나: 토니가 털이 많나요?

제프: 그럴 거예요.

티나: 토니가 호랑이인가요? 호랑이가 도망친 건가요?

제프: 네! 하지만 조용히 해 주세요! 저는 곤란해지고 싶지 않아요. 동물원이 개장하기 전에 토니를 찾아야만 해요.

티나: 음, 알았어요, 그렇게 해요.

제프: 저를 도와주실 수 있나요?

티나: 물론이죠. 어떻게 이런 일이 일어났는지 말씀해 주시겠어요?

제프: 글쎄, 제가 호랑이 우리를 청소하려고 문을 열었는데 그 호랑이가 나를 쓰러뜨리고 도망갔어요.

티나: 오, 이런! 그 호랑이가 어디로 갔는지 봤어요?

제프: 제 생각에 이쪽으로 간 것 같은데, 더는 보이지 않네요.

티나: 그가 어디에 있을 수 있을까요?

제프: 잘 모르겠어요. 아침을 먹어서 배가 부를 거예요. 어이쿠, 오늘 너무 덥네요!

티나: 바로 그거예요!

제프: 그게 뭐죠?

티나: 오늘 너무 덥고 호랑이는 물을 좋아해요. 그는 연못에 있을 거예요.

제프: 티나 말이 맞을지도 몰라요!

티나: 보세요, 저기에 있네요! 어서 잡아요!

ESCAPED ANIMAL AT THE ZOO

Tina: Hey, Jeff! How are you today?

Jeff: I'm good. Actually, have you seen Tony?

Tina: Who is Tony? What does he look like?

Jeff: Tony lives here. He's orange and white with black stripes and he weighs about five hundred pounds.

Tina: He's pretty heavy! Wait... orange and white with black stripes?

Jeff: Yes.

Tina: Is Tony furry?

Jeff: Maybe.

Tina: Is Tony a tiger? Did our tiger escape?

Jeff: Yes! But keep it down! I don't want to get in trouble. We have to find Tony before the zoo opens.

Tina: Umm, yes, we do.

Jeff: Will you help me?

Tina: Sure. Can you tell me how this happened?

Jeff: Well, I opened the door to clean his enclosure but he knocked me over and ran away.

Tina: Oh, no! Did you see where he went?

Jeff: I think he went this way, but I don't see him anymore.

Tina: Where could he be?

Jeff: I'm not sure. He should be full from breakfast. Gosh, it's so hot today!

Tina: That's it!

Jeff: What's it?

Tina: It's so hot today and tigers like the water. I bet he's at the pond.

Jeff: You may be right!

Tina: Look, there he is! Hurry up and catch him!

54

캠핑 여행
-
CAMPING TRIP (A2)

피터: 저 소리 들었어?

그웬: 아니.

피터: 밖에서 무슨 소리가 난 것 같아.

그웬: 어디서?

피터: 저기 나무에서 소리가 난 것 같은데.

그웬: 소리가 어떻게 들리는 데?

피터: 뭔가 터지는 것 같은 소리였어.

그웬: 불 아니야? 난 불 타는 소리를 계속 듣고 있었어.

피터: 네가 아마도 맞을 거야.

그웬: 나 겁주지마.

피터: 미안해.

그웬: 배고프다.

피터: 핫도그가 다 된 것 같아. 빵은 가져왔어?

그웬: 응, 여기 있어. 핫도그 맛있게 보인다!

피터: 응! 여기, 이건 네 거야.

그웬: 고마워. 케첩 필요해?

피터: 아니, 머스타드 소스만 줘. 고마워.

그웬: 머스타드는 안 가져 왔어. 미안!

피터: 괜찮아. 물은 있어?

그웬: 응, 여기 있어.

피터: 숲이 아름다워.

그웬: 응 나도 그렇게 생각해. 숲에서 캠핑하는 거 정말 좋아.

피터: 아침에 해돋이를 보고 싶어.

그웬: 나도. 해돋이는 아침 여섯 시니까 엄청 일찍 일어나야 해.

피터: 네 말이 맞아. 자러 가자.

그웬: 알았어, 텐트는 가져왔어?

피터: 당연하지! 나 좀 도와줄 수 있어?

그웬: 물론이지!

CAMPING TRIP

Peter: Did you hear that?

Gwen: No.

Peter: I think I heard something out there.

Gwen: Where?

Peter: I think the noise was coming from those trees.

Gwen: What did the noise sound like?

Peter: It sounded like something popped.

Gwen: Are you sure it wasn't the fire? I've been listening to the fire making popping noises.

Peter: You're probably right.

Gwen: Don't scare me like that.

Peter: I'm sorry.

Gwen: I'm getting hungry.

Peter: I think the hotdogs are ready. Did you bring the buns?

Gwen: Yeah, they're right here. Those hotdogs look really good!

Peter: Yeah! Here, this one is yours.

Gwen: Thank you. Do you want some ketchup?

Peter: No, just mustard, please.

Gwen: I didn't bring any mustard. Sorry!

Peter: That's okay. Do you have any water?

Gwen: Yes, here you go.

Peter: This is a lovely forest.

Gwen: I think so, too. I love camping in the forest.

Peter: I want to watch the sunrise in the morning.

Gwen: Me too. Sunrise is at 6 a.m., so we need to wake up very early.

Peter: You're right. Let's go to bed.

Gwen: Okay, did you bring the tent?

Peter: Of course! Can you help me with it?

Gwen: Sure!

55

가장 친한 친구의 가족

-

MY BEST FRIEND'S FAMILY (A2)

클라우스: 이번 주에 뭐 할 거야?

비비아나: 아직 모르겠어. 너는?

클라우스: 내 친구 아담네 가족이랑 여행을 갈 거야.

비비아나: 아, 진짜? 아담네 가족들이랑 가까워?

클라우스: 응, 내 두 번째 가족과도 같아.

비비아나: 너무 좋다. 뭐 할 거야?

클라우스: 아담의 집이 호수 옆에 있어서 거기에 갈 거야.

비비아나: 멋지다! 아담이랑 친구가 된 지 얼마나 됐어?

클라우스: 십이 년 정도. 초등학교에서 만났어.

비비아나: 와. 아담은 형제나 자매가 있어?

클라우스: 응. 여동생이 하나 있어.

비비아나: 몇 살이야?

클라우스: 열여섯 살. 아직 고등학생이야.

비비아나: 그렇구나. 여동생도 호수에 가는 거야?

클라우스: 그럴거야. 아담 여동생이 내 동생이랑도 친구야. 그래서 우리는 꼭 대가족 같아!

비비아나: 우와! 완벽하네.

클라우스: 응.

비비아나: 네 동생도 이번 주에 거기 가는 거야?

클라우스: 아니, 걔는 수능 공부해야 해.

비비아나: 아, 그렇구나.

클라우스: 내 동생은 우리가 자기 없이 가는 걸 질투하고 있어.

비비아나: 그래도, 동생이 시험을 잘 치고 두 가족이 함께 축하할 수 있기를 바랄게!

클라우스: 응! 그거 좋은 생각이야.

MY BEST FRIEND'S FAMILY

Klaus: What will you do this weekend?

Viviana: I don't know yet. What about you?

Klaus: I am going on a trip with my friend Adam's family.

Viviana: Oh, really? Are you close to his family?

Klaus: Yes, they're like my second family.

Viviana: That's so nice. What will you do?

Klaus: They have a house by the lake. So, we are going there.

Viviana: Cool! How many years have you been friends with Adam?

Klaus: About twelve years. We met in elementary school.

Viviana: Aww. Does Adam have siblings?

Klaus: Yes. He has a younger sister.

Viviana: How old is she?

Klaus: She's sixteen. She's still in high school.

Viviana: I see. Will she go to the lake, too?

Klaus: I think so. She's also friends with my sister. So, it's like we're one big family!

Viviana: Oh, wow! That's perfect.

Klaus: It is.

Viviana: Will your sister be there this weekend?

Klaus: No, she has to study for the SATs.

Viviana: Oh, I see.

Klaus: She's really jealous that we are going without her.

Viviana: Well, hopefully she gets a good score and then both of your families can celebrate together!

Klaus: Yes! That's a good idea.

56

축구 부상
-
A SOCCER INJURY (A2)

로건: 병원에 가야 할 것 같아.

미아: 왜?

로건: 축구 시합을 하다가 발을 다쳤어.

미아: 오, 이런! 어쩌다가 다친거야?

로건: 내가 공을 드리블하고 있었는데 상대편 남자가 내 발을 밟았어. 처음에는 그렇게 아프지 않았는데 좀 지나고 나니까 너무 아프더라고. 그래서 코치에게 말해서 코치가 나를 게임에서 빼줬어. 부러진 건 아닌 거 같은 데 뭔가 잘못된 것 같아.

미아: 걸어 다닐 수 있어?

로건: 조금, 그런데 발에 무게를 많이 싣지는 못 하겠어.

미아: 얼음 올려 봤어?

로건: 아니, 아직.

미아: 얼음 찜질하는 게 좋아. 내 친구 케이티가 간호사인데, 걔한테 전화해 볼게.

로건: 알았어, 고마워.

(오 분 후...)

미아: 케이티가 그러는데, 발에 얼음 찜질하고 걷지 말래. 오늘 응급실에 가보는 게 좋을 거래.

로건: 으윽, 알았어.

미아: 내가 두 시 삼십 분에 차로 데려다줄 수 있어.

로건: 고마워! 거기서 같이 기다릴 필요는 없고, 그냥 데려다 주기만 해 줘.

미아: 기다려도 괜찮아. 학교때문에 읽어야 할 게 많아.

로건: 정말이야?

미아: 응, 걱정하지 마! 이따가 봐.

로건: 너무 고마워! 두 시 반에 봐.

A SOCCER INJURY

Logan: I think I should go to the hospital.

Mia: Why?

Logan: I hurt my foot playing soccer.

Mia: Oh, no! What happened?

Logan: I was dribbling the ball and a guy on the other team stepped on my foot. It didn't really hurt at first, but then a few minutes later I was in a lot of pain. So, I told my coach and he took me out of the game. I don't think it's broken, but something is wrong.

Mia: Can you walk on it?

Logan: A little, but I don't want to put too much weight on my foot.

Mia: Have you put ice on it?

Logan: No, not yet.

Mia: You should ice it. I'll call my friend Katie who's a nurse.

Logan: Okay, thanks.

(Five minutes later...)

Mia: Katie said to ice the foot and don't walk on it. She said you should try to go to urgent care today.

Logan: Ugh, all right.

Mia: I can drive you there at two thirty.

Logan: Thanks! You don't have to wait there with me. You can just drop me off.

Mia: I don't mind waiting. I have a lot of reading to do for school.

Logan: Are you sure?

Mia: Yeah, no worries! I'll see you soon.

Logan: Thanks so much! I'll see you at two thirty.

57

교통 체증

-

STUCK IN TRAFFIC (A2)

아바: 앞에 빨간 불이 켜진 게 왜 그렇게 많은 거야?

대니: 차가 막힌 것 같아.

아바: 으윽, 차 막히는 거 싫은데! 심지어 교통 혼잡 시간도 아니잖아.

대니: 사고가 있었나 봐.

아바: 그럴 수도. 네 휴대폰으로 교통 정보 좀 찾아봐 줄래?

대니: 물론이지. 앱에서는 다음 십 마일까지 차가 막힐 거래.

아바: 십 마일?! 오래 걸리네!

대니: 응, 근데 오 마일 정도만 많이 혼잡하고 그 뒤로는 좀 나아질 듯해. 사고가 있었던 것 같아.

아바: 그러게, 다친 사람이 없어야 할텐데.

대니: 그러게. 사실, 내가 지름길을 찾은 것 같아.

아바: 진짜?

대니: 응. 지도 앱을 보고 있는데 교통 체증을 피할 수 있는 길이 있어.

아바: 좋아!

대니: 하지만 그 길로 가기 전에 삼 마일 정도는 차가 막힐 거야.

아바: 괜찮아. 그건 감당할 수 있어.

대니: 좋았어, 여기서 나가자!

아바: 알았어. 그러고 나서는?

대니: 일 마일을 직진하다가 헤드웨이 플레이스에서 우회전해. 그 후에 십삼 마일을 직진하면 도착할 거야!

아바: 그러면 우리 교통 체증은 피하는 거네!

대니: 맞아.

STUCK IN TRAFFIC

Ava: Why are there so many red lights up ahead?

Danny: It looks like a traffic jam.

Ava: Ugh, I hate traffic! It's not even rush hour.

Danny: Maybe there was an accident.

Ava: Maybe. Can you try to find information about the traffic on your phone?

Danny: Sure. According to the app, there will be traffic for another ten miles.

Ava: Ten miles?! That's a long time!

Danny: Yes, but the traffic is only heavy for about five miles. After that it gets a little better. I think there was an accident.

Ava: Well, I hope everyone is okay.

Danny: Me too. Actually, I think I found a shortcut.

Ava: Really?

Danny: Yeah. I'm looking at my maps app. There is a route we can take that will help us avoid the traffic.

Ava: Great!

Danny: But we will be stuck in traffic for another three miles before we can take the other route.

Ava: That's okay. I can deal with it.

Danny: All right, exit here!

Ava: Okay. Then what?

Danny: Go straight for one mile, then turn right on Headway Place. After that, we go straight for thirteen miles, and then we arrive!

Ava: And we skip the traffic!

Danny: Yep.

58

당신은 해고됐습니다

-

YOU'RE FIRED (A2)

알렉시스: 안녕하세요, 데이비드. 제 사무실에서 볼 수 있을까요? 데이비드 씨와 이야기를 하고 싶은 것이 있습니다.

데이비드: 네, 그럼요.

알렉시스: 데이비드 씨의 근태에 관해서 이야기를 하고 싶습니다. 데이비드 씨가 최근에 일곱 번에서 여덟 번 십 분 이상 지각했습니다. 저희가 이 부분에 대해서 말씀을 드렸었고, 데이비드 씨가 시간을 지키겠다고 약속을 했었습니다. 하지만 데이비드 씨가 지각을 여전히 하고 있습니다. 계속해서 늦으시면, 저희는 당신을 해고할 수 밖에 없습니다.

데이비드: 정말로 죄송해요. 저와 함께 사는 세 명의 룸메이트들이 항상 파티를 열어요. 너무 시끄러워서 가끔 제가 잠을 잘 수가 없더라고요. 그리고 가끔 저도 파티에 가는데, 제가 이 도시로 이사 온 지 얼마 되지 않기도 하고 사람들과 만나서 즐겁게 놀고 싶더라고요.

알렉시스: 사람들을 만나 즐겁게 놀고 싶은 건 이해하지만 이건 데이비드 씨 일입니다. 시간을 잘 지키는 것이 중요해요.

데이비드: 여덟 시 말고 여덟 시 반에 출근하면 안될까요? 그리고 다섯 시 대신 다섯 시 반까지 있는 건요?

알렉시스: 안됩니다, 데이비드 씨. 저희 직원들은 여덟 시에 도착해야만 합니다.

데이비드: 그건 공평하지 않다고 생각해요. 저는 일도 열심히 하고 회사를 많이 돕고 있다고요.

알렉시스: 네. 하지만 규칙은 지켜야죠. 저기 데이비드 씨... 태도가 별로 좋지 않네요. 저희는 시간을 엄수하고 책임감이 있는 직원이 필요합니다. 이번 주 금요일 이후로는 나오지 않으셔도 됩니다.

데이비드: 뭐라고요?!

알렉시스: 죄송합니다, 데이비드. 더 이상은 여기서 일하실 수 없습니다.

YOU'RE FIRED

Alexis: Hi, David. Can I see you in my office? I want to talk to you about something.

David: Yeah, no problem.

Alexis: I want to talk to you about your tardiness. You have been more than ten minutes late seven or eight times recently. We talked to you about it and you promised to be punctual. But you are still coming to work late. If you continue to be late, we will have to terminate you.

David: I'm really sorry. I have three roommates and they always have parties. Sometimes I can't sleep because it's so loud. And sometimes I go to the parties because I just moved to this city and I want to meet people and have fun.

Alexis: I understand that you want to meet people and have fun, but this is your job. It's important that you are punctual.

David: Can I just arrive at work at eight thirty instead of eight o'clock? And then stay until five thirty instead of five o'clock?

Alexis: No, David. Our employees must arrive at eight o'clock.

David: I don't think that's fair. I work hard and I have helped the company a lot.

Alexis: Yes. But you have to respect the rules. You know, David... your attitude is not very good. We need employees that are punctual and responsible. This Friday will be your last day.

David: What?!

Alexis: I'm sorry, David. You can't work here anymore.

59

나의 서른 번째 생일

-

MY THIRTIETH BIRTHDAY (A2)

다니엘라: 안녕, 놀란!

놀란: 안녕, 다니엘라!

다니엘라: 금요일 밤에 계획 있어?

놀란: 금요일에 오후 일곱 시까지 일해. 왜?

다니엘라: 이번 주가 내 생일이어서 금요일에 파티를 할 거야.

놀란: 오, 좋다! 파티가 몇 시야?

다니엘라: 오후 여섯 시쯤. 근데 늦게 도착해도 괜찮아! 우리는 레스토랑에 갔다가 저녁 먹고 술집에 갈 거야. 술집에서 만나면 되겠어.

놀란: 알았어! 나도 가고 싶어. 오랫동안 너 못 봤잖아!

다니엘라: 맞아! 잘 지내고 있어?

놀란: 잘 지내. 그냥 일 때문에 바빠.

다니엘라: 안나는 어때?

놀란: 잘 지내. 안나가 새 직장을 마음에 들어 해

다니엘라: 멋지네.

놀란: 그건 그렇고, 어떤 레스토랑에 가는 거야?

다니엘라: 얼반 피자리아. 거기 가본 적 있어?

놀란: 아니, 내 친구가 가 봤는데 완전 좋다고 했어.

다니엘라: 아싸.

놀란: 그리고 나서 술집은 어디로 가?

다니엘라: 아직 확실하지 않지만, 내가 알려줄게!

놀란: 좋아. 이번 주말에 봐! 아, 몇 번째 생일이야?

다니엘라: 서른 번째 생일이야. 공식적으로 나이가 든 거지!

놀란: 아니야 안그래! 그리고 너 아직 스물 한 살처럼 보여.

다니엘라: 우와. 고마워! 내가 금요일에 술 한 잔 사 줄게.

놀란: 하하, 알았어!

MY THIRTIETH BIRTHDAY

Daniela: Hi, Nolan!

Nolan: Hey, Daniela!

Daniela: Do you have plans on Friday night?

Nolan: I work until 7 p.m. on Friday. Why?

Daniela: It's my birthday this weekend and I'm having a party on Friday.

Nolan: Oh, cool! What time is the party?

Daniela: Around 6:00 p.m. But if you get there late, it's okay! We are going to a restaurant and then a bar after we finish dinner. You can meet us at the bar.

Nolan: Okay! I would love to go. I haven't seen you in a long time!

Daniela: I know! How is everything going?

Nolan: It's good. Just busy with work.

Daniela: How's Ana?

Nolan: She's great. She loves her new job.

Daniela: Awesome.

Nolan: So, which restaurant are you going to?

Daniela: Urban Pizzeria. Have you been there?

Nolan: No, but my friend went there and said it was really good.

Daniela: Yay.

Nolan: And which bar are you going to later?

Daniela: I'm not sure yet, but I will let you know!

Nolan: Sounds good. I'll see you this weekend! Oh, and which birthday is this?

Daniela: It's my thirtieth. I'm officially old!

Nolan: No you're not! And you still look like you're twenty-one.

Daniela: Oh, wow. Thank you! I'm buying you a drink on Friday.

Nolan: Ha ha, okay!

60

그건 내거야

-

THAT'S MINE (A2)

마티아스: 내가 뭘 찾았는지 봐! 내가 좋아하는 티셔츠야! 이거 두 달 전에 잃어버렸거든

잭클린: 그건 내 티셔츠야.

마티아스: 아니야... 이거 내 거야.

잭클린: 네가 그 티셔츠 나한테 줬었잖아.

마티아스: 아니, 안 줬어. 네 잠옷이 전부 더러웠을 때 네가 이거 입고 자고 싶대서 내가 너한테 빌려줬던 거야. 그리고 이게 사라졌지.

잭클린: 나는 네가 나한테 영원히 주는 줄 알았어.

마티아스: 아니야! 나 이 셔츠 좋아해. 그냥 빌려줬던 거야.

잭클린: 아...

마티아스: 티셔츠를 소파 뒤에서 찾았어. 그게 어떻게 거기 들어간 거지?

잭클린: 몰라. 우리 청소를 좀 더 자주 해야 할 것 같아!

마티아스: 맞아.

잭클린: 그리고... 그 셔츠 나 주면 안돼?

마티아스: 안돼! 내가 제일 좋아하는 티셔츠란 말이야.

잭클린: 같이 입으면 안돼?

마티아스: 가끔가다 한 번은 입어도 괜찮아. 하지만 나한테 먼저 물어봐야 해.

잭클린: 하하, 진짜?

마티아스: 응! 너는 티셔츠 도둑이야.

잭클린: 알았어, 좋아.

THAT'S MINE

Mathias: Look what I found! My favorite T-shirt! I lost this two months ago.

Jacklyn: That's my T-shirt.

Mathias: No... it's mine.

Jacklyn: You gave that shirt to me.

Mathias: No, I didn't. I lent it to you because you wanted to wear it to bed when all your other pajamas were dirty. And then it disappeared.

Jacklyn: I thought you were giving it to me forever.

Mathias: No! I love this shirt. I was just letting you borrow it.

Jacklyn: Oh...

Mathias: I found it behind the sofa. How did it get back there?

Jacklyn: I don't know. I think we need to clean more often!

Mathias: Yeah.

Jacklyn: So... can I have the shirt?

Mathias: No! It's my favorite T-shirt.

Jacklyn: Can we share it?

Mathias: You can wear it once in a while. But you have to ask me first.

Jacklyn: Ha ha, really?

Mathias: Yes! You're a T-shirt thief.

Jacklyn: Okay, fine.

61

초록 엄지손가락

-

A GREEN THUMB (A2)

리치: 안녕하세요, 마리안 씨.

마리안: 안녕하세요, 리치 씨. 오늘 기분이 어떠세요?

리치: 매우 좋아요. 마리안 씨는요?

마리안: 좋아요. 식물에 물 주고 있었어요.

리치: 사실 마리안 씨 식물에 대해서 이야기를 하고 싶었어요.

마리안: 아, 진짜요?

리치: 네. 제가 가족들이랑 이 주 동안 여행을 갈건데, 저희가 없는 동안 마리안 씨가 저희 식물에 물을 주실 수 있는지 여쭤보고 싶었어요.

마리안: 물론이죠! 좋아하는 이웃을 도울 수 있어 기쁘네요.

리치: 정말 감사합니다! 저는 식물을 잘 못 길러요. 식물에 물과 빛을 얼마나 많이 줘야 하는지 전혀 알지 못해요. 식물들이 항상 죽더라고요.

마리안: 오 이런! 그렇다면, 리치 씨께 식물에 대해 조금 가르쳐 줄 수 있어서 기쁘네요. 사람들이 제가 초록색 엄지를 가졌다고 말하거든요.

리치: 무슨 뜻이에요? 마리안 씨의 엄지손가락은 초록색이 아닌데요.

마리안: 하하. 실제로 초록색이라는 의미가 아니에요. "초록색 엄지손가락"은 식물을 잘 돌본다는 얘기예요.

리치: 아! 한 번도 못 들어본 이야기네요.

마리안: 정말요?!

리치: 정말요.

마리안: 그렇다면, 이제 이 표현을 아시겠네요! 그리고 제가 리치 씨에게 식물에 대해 가르쳐 드리고 나면, 아마 리치 씨 손가락도 초록색으로 변할 거예요!

리치: 그러길 바래요! 제 아내가 저는 식물을 항상 죽인대요. 저희 식물이 살아있다면 아내가 행복해 할 거예요.

마리안: 리치 씨네 식물들도 행복할 거예요!

A GREEN THUMB

Rich: Hi, Maryann.

Maryann: Hello, Rich! How are you today?

Rich: I'm great. How are you?

Maryann: I'm good. I'm just watering my plants.

Rich: I actually wanted to talk to you about your plants.

Maryann: Oh really?

Rich: Yes. My family and I are taking a trip for two weeks, and I wanted to ask you if you can water our plants while we are gone.

Maryann: Of course! I'm always happy to help my favorite neighbors.

Rich: Thanks so much! I am so bad with plants. I never know how much water or light to give them. They always die.

Maryann: Oh no! Well, I'm happy to teach you a little about plants. People say I have a green thumb.

Rich: What do you mean? Your thumb isn't green.

Maryann: Ha ha. No, I don't mean it's *actually* green. "A green thumb" means you are good at taking care of plants.

Rich: Oh! I've never heard that before.

Maryann: Really?!

Rich: Really.

Maryann: Well, now you know that expression! And after I teach you about plants, maybe your thumb will turn green, too!

Rich: I hope so! My wife says I always kill our plants. She will be happy if our plants stay alive.

Maryann: I'm sure your plants will be happy, too!

62

너의 완벽한 하루

-

YOUR PERFECT DAY (A2)

지환: 게임 하자.

줄리엣: 게임? 무슨 게임?

지환: 눈을 감고 너의 완벽한 하루를 상상해 봐.

줄리엣: 눈은 왜 감아야 해?

지환: 왜냐하면 그래야 상상이 더 잘되거든.

줄리엣: 알았어.

지환: 좋아, 그럼 너의 하루는 어떻게 시작해?

줄리엣: 잠에서 깨면 나는 발리에 있는 아주 멋진 집에서 매우 편안한 침대에 누워 있어.

지환: 발리! 좋네. 그런 다음에는?

줄리엣: 침실 밖에서 폭포 소리가 들리고 새들은 지저귀고 있어. 나는 밖으로 걸어 나가서 아름다운 경치를 봐. 내 개인 수영장이 있고 그 너머에는 열대 우림이 있어. 그리고 내 주변에는 나비들이 날아다니고 있어.

지환: 정말 아름답게 들리네. 이제 뭐 해?

줄리엣: 잘생긴 남자가 내게 아침을 가져다줘.

지환: 잠깐, 나 말고 다른 잘생긴 남자?

줄리엣: 잘생긴 남자라고 말했잖아.

지환: 너무하네!

줄리엣: 장난이야! 네가 "완벽한 하루"라며. 이게 내 완벽한 하루라고.

지환: 알았어, 좋아. 계속해 봐.

줄리엣: 잘생긴 남자가 내게 아침을 가져다줘. 아침은 맛있고 나는

그걸 즐기며 아름다운 경치를 보고 있어. 그때 아기 코끼리가 나에게 달려와서 우리는 함께 한 시간 동안 놀아.

지환: 우와.

줄리엣: 그 다음에 나는 집 주변에 있는 강과 폭포에서 수영을 해.

지환: 나는 거기 있어?

줄리엣: 응, 지금 너는 나와 함께 있어. 너가 자고 있었는데 아기 코끼리가 너를 깨웠어. 그러고 나서 우리는 온종일 해변과 정글을 탐험해!

지환: 정말 멋지게 들려! 실제로 우리가 그렇게 할 수 있을까?

줄리엣: 응. 우리는 먼저 돈을 더 많이 벌어야 해!

지환: 하하, 알았어! 이제 동기 부여가 되네!

YOUR PERFECT DAY

Ji-hwan: Let's play a game.

Juliette: A game? What kind of game?

Ji-hwan: Close your eyes and imagine your perfect day.

Juliette: Why do I need to close my eyes?

Ji-hwan: Because it will help you imagine it better.

Juliette: Okay.

Ji-hwan: All right, so how do you begin your day?

Juliette: I wake up, and I am in a super comfortable bed in an amazing house in Bali.

Ji-hwan: Bali! Cool. Then what?

Juliette: I hear the sound of a waterfall outside my bedroom, and the birds are chirping. I walk outside and I see a beautiful view. I have a private pool and behind my private pool there is a rainforest. And there are butterflies flying around me.

Ji-hwan: That sounds beautiful. What do you do now?

Juliette: A handsome man delivers breakfast to me.

Ji-hwan: Wait—me or a different handsome man?

Juliette: I said a *handsome* man.

Ji-hwan: That's mean!

Juliette: I'm kidding! You said "perfect day" and this is my perfect day.

Ji-hwan: Okay, fine. Continue.

Juliette: A handsome man delivers breakfast to me. It's delicious and I'm enjoying it and looking at the beautiful scenery. Then a baby elephant runs over to me and we play for an hour.

Ji-hwan: Wow.

Juliette: And then I swim in the river and the waterfall near my house.

Ji-hwan: Am I there?

Juliette: Yes, now you're with me. You were sleeping but the baby elephant woke you up. Then we explore beaches and jungles all day!

Ji-hwan: That sounds amazing! Can we do that in real life?

Juliette: Yes. We just need to make a lot more money first!

Ji-hwan: Ha ha, okay! Now I'm motivated!

63

당신은 어떤 언어를 배우고 싶나요?

-

WHAT LANGUAGE DO YOU WANT TO LEARN? (A2)

바네사: 몇 개 언어를 할 줄 아세요, 제이 씨?

제이: 영어만 할 줄 알아요. 스페인어는 고등학교 때 배워서 조금 알아요. 바네사 씨는요?

바네사: 저는 영어와 스페인어를 하고 중학교와 고등학교에서 프랑스어를 공부했어요.

제이: 우와! 프랑스어는 배우기가 어려웠나요?

바네사: 별로요. 스페인어와 비슷해요.

제이: 네, 일리가 있네요. 스페인어와 영어도 비슷해요.

바네사: 사실이에요. 그게 영어와 중국어에 비하면 더 비슷해요, 예를 들어서 말이죠!

제이: 네, 훨씬 더 비슷해요! 사실, 저는 중국어를 배우고 싶어요.

바네사: 진짜요? 왜요?

제이: 글쎄요, 저는 사업가가 되고 싶은데 중국어가 미래에 매우 유용할 것 같아요. 중국어가 점점 더 멀리 퍼지고 있거든요.

바네사: 네, 그래요. 하지만 중국어는 배우기 너무 어려워요, 그렇죠?

제이: 네. 매우 어려워요. 특히 읽기, 쓰기, 발음이 그래요.

바네사: 어떻게 공부하고 있으세요?

제이: 교재로 공부하기도 하고 인터넷에서 중국 텔레비전 쇼를 보기도 해요.

바네사: 정말 멋지네요! 언제부터 중국어를 배우기 시작하셨어요?

제이: 석 달 전쯤에요. 저는 아직 초보자예요. 그래도 몇 가지 문장을 말할 수 있어서 행복해요.

바네사: 멋있어요! 그리고 중국어를 공부하는 것이 좋은 생각인 것 같아요. 제이 씨가 취직할 때 회사가 제이 씨 지원서에 관심을 가질 거예요.

제이: 그러길 바래요. 어떤 언어를 배우고 싶어요?

바네사: 이탈리아어를 배우고 싶어요. 너무 아름다운 것 같아요.

제이: 동의해요! 이탈리아어를 공부하면 좋을 거예요.

바네사: 사실, 제이 씨에게 영감을 받고 있어요. 저는 이제 이탈리아어를 배우기 시작할 거예요!

제이: 좋아요!

WHAT LANGUAGE DO YOU WANT TO LEARN?

Vanessa: How many languages do you speak, Jay?

Jay: Just English. I studied Spanish in high school so I know a little bit of it. What about you?

Vanessa: I speak English and Spanish, and I studied French in middle school and high school.

Jay: Oh, wow! Was French hard for you to learn?

Vanessa: Not really. It's similar to Spanish.

Jay: Yeah, that makes sense. Spanish and English are similar, too.

Vanessa: True. They are more similar than English and Chinese, for example!

Jay: Yes, much more similar! Actually, I want to learn Chinese.

Vanessa: Really? Why?

Jay: Well, I want to be a businessman, and I think Chinese will be very useful in the future. It is becoming more widespread.

Vanessa: Yes, it is. But Chinese is very difficult to learn, right?

Jay: Yeah. It's very hard. Especially reading, writing, and pronunciation.

Vanessa: How are you studying?

Jay: I have a textbook and I watch some Chinese TV shows on the Internet.

Vanessa: That's so cool! When did you start learning Chinese?

Jay: About three months ago. I'm still a beginner. But I can say a few sentences, so I'm happy about that.

Vanessa: That's awesome! And I think it's a good idea to study Chinese. When you apply for jobs, the companies will be interested in your application.

Jay: I hope so. What language do you want to learn?

Vanessa: I want to learn Italian. I think it's so beautiful.

Jay: I agree! You should study Italian.

Vanessa: Actually, you are inspiring me. I think I will start learning it now!

Jay: Great!

64

넌 너무 많은 신발을 갖고 있어!

-

YOU HAVE TOO MANY SHOES! (A2)

브랜든: 스테파니, 옷장이 너무 꽉 찼어! 내 옷 넣을 공간이 없잖아.

스테파니: 이런. 미안해. 내가 신발이 많아.

브랜든: 넌 신발이 너무 많아! 신발을 몇 켤레나 갖고 있는 거야?

스테파니: 음... 지난달에 서른네 켤레였는데 지난주에 또 한 켤레를 샀지 뭐야.

브랜든: 그러면, 너는 신발이 서른다섯 켤레나 있는 거야?!

스테파니: 응.

브랜든: 정말 신발이 서른다섯 켤레나 필요해?

스테파니: 신발이 정말 좋아. 그리고 거의 다 신는 거야.

브랜든: 다 신지는 않잖아. 너는 신발 몇 개를 자선 단체에 기부하는 게 좋을 것 같아.

스테파니: 네 말이 맞아. 지금 신발을 전부 살펴보고 어떤 신발을 남겨 둘지 결정할게.

브랜든: 정말 좋은 생각인 것 같아. 도와줄까?

스테파니: 응.

브랜든: 알았어.... 이 보라색 신발은 어때?

스테파니: 정말 좋아해! 작년 이자벨 결혼식과 회사 파티에서 그 신발을 신었어.

브랜든: 그래서 딱 두 번만 신었다는 거야?

스테파니: 응.

브랜든: 이 신발 언제 또 신을 거야?

스테파니: 모르겠어. 아마도 내년에.

브랜든: 내년에?! 너 정말 이 신발을 옷장에 일 년 동안 보관하고 싶어? 이 신발을 자선 단체에 기부하면 다른 사람이 신을 수 있잖아.

스테파니: 응. 네 말이 맞아. 잘 가, 보라색 신발. 너를 신는 건 즐거웠어!

브랜든: 잘했어, 스테파니! 좋아, 이 파란색 운동화는 어때...?

YOU HAVE TOO MANY SHOES!

Brandon: Steph, the closet is so full! There is no space for my clothes.

Stephanie: Oops. I'm sorry. I have a lot of shoes.

Brandon: You have too many shoes! And how many pairs of shoes do you have?

Stephanie: Umm... I had thirty-four last month. But I bought another pair last week.

Brandon: So, you have thirty-five pairs of shoes?!

Stephanie: Yes.

Brandon: Do you really need thirty-five pairs of shoes?

Stephanie: I really like shoes. And I wear most of them.

Brandon: But you don't wear all of them. You should donate some of your shoes to charity.

Stephanie: You're right. I will look at all my shoes now and decide which ones I want to keep.

Brandon: I think that's a really good idea. Do you want some help?

Stephanie: Sure.

Brandon: Okay.... what about these purple ones?

Stephanie: I love those! I wore those to Isabelle's wedding and to my office party last year.

Brandon: So, you only wore them two times?

Stephanie: Yes.

Brandon: When will you wear them again?

Stephanie: I don't know. Maybe next year.

Brandon: Next year?! Do you really want to keep these in the closet for a year? If you give them to charity, another person can wear them.

Stephanie: Yeah. You're right. Bye, purple shoes. I enjoyed wearing you!

Brandon: Good job, Steph! Okay, what about these blue sneakers...?

65

별로 좋은 말이 아니야

-

THAT'S NOT VERY NICE (A2)

아리안나: 크리스토퍼! 네 여동생을 "바보"라고 부르지 마! 좋은 말이 아니야.

크리스토퍼: 하지만 제 공을 가져갔어요!!

아리안나: 음, 그건 동생이 나빴어. 하지만 동생을 바보라고 불러서는 안 돼. 좋은 단어가 아니야.

크리스토퍼: 상관없어요. 걔한테 화가 난 걸요.

아리안나: 동생한테 미안하다고 하렴.

크리스토퍼: 싫어요.

아리안나: 크리스토퍼, 내 말 들어. 동생한테 사과해.

크리스토퍼: 나중에 할게요.

아리안나: 지금 하렴.

크리스토퍼: 알았어요. 케이트, 미안해.

아리안나: 뭐가 미안한데? 동생한테 말해줘.

크리스토퍼: 내가 너를 바보라고 불러서 미안해.

아리안나: 고마워, 크리스토퍼. 케이트가 하는 말 들었어? 케이트도 너한테 방금 미안하다고 했어.

크리스토퍼: 알았어요. 동생들은 너무 짜증 나요.

아리안나: 동생들은 멋진 거야. 내 언니는 가장 친한 친구야. 우리도 어렸을 때는 많이 싸웠는데 지금은 언니한테 정말 고마워.

크리스토퍼: 엄마랑 크리스티나 이모랑 무슨 일로 싸웠는데요?

아리안나: 전부다. 보통 아이들이 싸우는 이유들이지.

크리스토퍼: 이모가 엄마 장난감을 가져간 적이 있어요?

아리안나: 물론이지.

크리스토퍼: 어떻게 했어요?

아리안나: 너무 화가 나서 너의 이모에게 가끔 나쁜 말을 했어. 하지만 그때 우리 엄마가 서로에게 미안하다고 말하라고 하셨어. 그리고 우리는 기분이 나아졌어.

크리스토퍼: 저는 기분이 나아지지 않아요.

아리안나: 아직은 아닐지도 몰라. 근데 그렇게 될 거야.

크리스토퍼: 알았어요. 저 지금 밖에 나가서 놀아도 돼요?

아리안나: 응. 하지만 저녁이 삼십 분 안에 준비될 거야.

크리스토퍼: 알겠어요. 고마워요, 엄마.

아리안나: 당연하지, 얘야.

THAT'S NOT VERY NICE

Arianna: Kristoffer! Don't call your sister "stupid"! That's not very nice.

Kristoffer: But she took my ball!

Arianna: Well, that was not nice of her. But you should not call her stupid. That's not a nice word.

Kristoffer: I don't care. I'm mad at her.

Arianna: Please tell her you're sorry.

Kristoffer: No.

Arianna: Kris, listen to me. Apologize to your sister.

Kristoffer: I'll do it later.

Arianna: Please do it now.

Kristoffer: Fine. Kate, I'm sorry.

Arianna: What are you sorry for? Tell her.

Kristoffer: I'm sorry I called you stupid.

Arianna: Thank you, Kris. And did you hear her? She just apologized to you, too.

Kristoffer: Okay. Sisters are so annoying.

Arianna: Sisters are wonderful. My sister is my best friend. When we were kids, we fought a lot. But now I am so grateful for her.

Kristoffer: What did you and Aunt Kristina fight about?

Arianna: Everything. Normal kid things.

Kristoffer: Did she ever take your toys?

Arianna: Of course.

Kristoffer: What did you do?

Arianna: I got angry at her and sometimes I said mean things to her. But then my mom told us to say I'm sorry to each other. And we felt better after.

Kristoffer: I don't feel better.

Arianna: Maybe not yet. But you will.

Kristoffer: Okay. Can I go play outside now?

Arianna: Yes. But dinner will be ready in half an hour.

Kristoffer: All right. Thanks, Mom.

Arianna: Of course, sweetie.

66

은행 계좌 개설하기

-

SETTING UP A BANK ACCOUNT (B1)

은행원: 안녕하세요! 어떻게 도와드릴까요?

제임스: 안녕하세요. 은행 계좌를 개설하려고요.

은행원: 좋아요! 제가 도와 드릴게요. 어떤 종류의 계좌를 개설하시겠어요?

제임스: 당좌 예금 계좌요.

은행원: 네. 당좌 예금 계좌만요? 보통 예금 계좌도 개설하시겠습니까?

제임스: 아니요, 당좌 예금 계좌만요.

은행원: 좋습니다. 계좌를 개설하려면 최소 이십오 달러를 입금해야 합니다.

제임스: 괜찮습니다. 더 많이 입금할 수 있나요?

은행원: 물론이죠! 이십오 달러만 넘으면 얼마든지 원하는 만큼의 액수로 시작할 수 있습니다.

제임스: 알겠습니다. 백 달러로 하겠습니다.

은행원: 좋습니다. 운전면허증과 주민등록번호가 필요합니다. 그리고 이 양식에 고객님의 기본 정보를 작성해 주세요.

제임스: 주민등록증을 없는데 괜찮나요? 번호는 알고요.

은행원: 괜찮습니다. 번호만 필요해요.

제임스: 알겠습니다. 직불 카드는 오늘 받을 수 있나요?

은행원: 아니요, 카드는 오 일에서 십 일 내에 우편으로 받으실겁니다.

제임스: 앗 그럼 직불 카드 받기 전에는 어떻게 결제하나요?

은행원: 이전 당좌 예금 계좌를 사용하거나 오늘 현금을 인출하셔서 카드를 받을 때까지 사용하시면 됩니다.

제임스: 알겠습니다. 도움 주셔서 감사합니다.

은행원: 감사합니다! 좋은 하루 보내세요!

제임스: 감사합니다. 좋은 하루 보내세요!

SETTING UP A BANK ACCOUNT

Bank employee: Hello! How can I help you?

James: Hi. I need to set up a bank account.

Bank employee: Great! I can help you with that. What kind of account would you like to open?

James: A checking account.

Bank employee: All right. Just a checking account? Would you like to open a savings account as well?

James: No, just a checking account.

Bank employee: Perfect. So, you'll need to deposit at least twenty-five dollars to open the account.

James: That's fine. Can I deposit more?

Bank employee: Yes, of course! You can start with however much you'd like, as long as it's over twenty-five dollars.

James: Okay. I'll start with one hundred dollars.

Bank employee: Sounds good. I'll need your driver's license and social security number. And you'll need to fill out this form with your basic information.

James: I don't have my social security card with me. Is that okay? But I know my number.

Bank employee: That's fine. We just need your number.

James: Okay. Do I get a debit card today?

Bank employee: No, it takes between five and ten days to receive your card. You'll get it in the mail.

James: Oh. How do I make purchases before I get my debit card?

Bank employee: You'll have to use your previous checking account, or you can withdraw some cash today and use that until you receive the card.

James: I see. All right, thanks for your help.

Bank employee: Thank you, too! Have a good day!

James: Thanks, you too.

67

비행기 탑승 기다리기

-

WAITING TO BOARD AN AIRPLANE (B1)

메이슨: 탑승은 언제 시작하는 거야?

알렉시스: 이제 시작해.

메이슨: 아, 알았어. 탑승권을 꺼내 놓는 게 좋겠어.

알렉시스: 맞아. 우리 좌석 번호가 뭐야?

메이슨: 사십칠 B 랑 사십칠 C 고, 중간이랑 통로 좌석이야.

알렉시스: 네가 통로 좌석에 앉고 싶으면 나는 가운데 좌석에 앉아도 괜찮아.

메이슨: 짧은 비행이니까 가운데도 진짜 상관없어.

알렉시스: 네가 다리가 기니까 통로 좌석에 앉아.

메이슨: 고마워! 시애틀에 도착하면 내가 마실 거 한 잔 살게.

알렉시스: 하하, 좋아!

메이슨: 줄이 기네. 비행기가 만석일 것 같아.

알렉시스: 네 말이 맞는 것 같아. 휴일 주말이니까 그럴 만해.

메이슨: 맞아. 기내 수화물 함에 가방 넣을 공간이 충분했으면 좋겠어. 우리가 가방을 부치지 않는 모험을 했잖아!

알렉시스: 맞아. 기내 가방을 끌고 다니는 건 좀 귀찮기는 해. 그런데 나는 가방을 내가 갖고 있는 것이 더 좋아. 그리고 수화물 찾는 곳에서 가방을 기다리는 걸 좋아하지 않아.

메이슨: 응. 가끔 가방이 나오는데 한참 걸릴 때도 있어. 도착하면 공항을 나가서 바로 여행을 시작하고 싶어!

알렉시스: 맞아. 나도 못 기다리겠어. 그래서 우리가 친구인가 봐!

메이슨: 하하. 그것이 많은 이유 중 하나지!

WAITING TO BOARD AN AIRPLANE

Mason: When does boarding start?

Alexis: It's starting now.

Mason: Oh, okay. We'd better get our boarding passes out.

Alexis: Yeah. What are our seat numbers?

Mason: 47B and 47C. Middle and aisle seats.

Alexis: I don't mind sitting in the middle if you want the aisle seat.

Mason: It's a short flight, so I really don't mind sitting in the middle.

Alexis: You have longer legs, so you can take the aisle.

Mason: Thanks! I'll buy you a drink when we land in Seattle.

Alexis: Ha ha, deal!

Mason: There are so many people in line; I think it will be a full flight.

Alexis: I think you're right. I'm not surprised; it's a holiday weekend.

Mason: Right. I hope there is enough space for our bags in the overhead bins. We took a risk by not checking our bags!

Alexis: I know. It's kind of a pain to lug around a carry-on bag, but I prefer to have my bag with me. And I don't like waiting for my bag at the baggage carousel.

Mason: Yeah. Sometimes it can take forever for the bags to come out! When I arrive I just want to get out of the airport and start my trip!

Alexis: Me too. I'm not patient, either. That must be why we're friends!

Mason: Ha ha. That's one of the many reasons!

68

개 입양
-
ADOPTING A DOG (B1)

웬디: 내 생각에 발리는 친구가 필요한 것 같아.

후안: 한 마리 더 데려오고 싶다고? 그럴 시간이 있어?

웬디: 응, 때가 된 것 같아.

후안: 알았어, 어떤 종류의 개를 데려올 생각이야?

웬디: 그건 잘 모르겠지만 한 마리를 입양하고 싶어. 보호소에 개들이 많아서 유기견을 입양하고 싶어.

후안: 하지만 개의 성격이 걱정되지 않아? 개가 사나우면 어떡해?

웬디: 내 친구가 유기견들을 데리고 있는데 다들 정말 사랑스러워. 그 유기견들이 자기들을 사랑이 넘치는 집에 데려와 줘서 고마워해. 그 사랑스러운 성격을 보면 알 수 있지.

후안: 그게 진짜인가 봐. 네 친구네 개 브리스켓도 매우 사랑스러워 보여. 그 개도 입양되었잖아.

웬디: 내말이!

후안: 그래서 어디에서 개를 입양할 거야? 보호소?

웬디: 응, 입양 센터나 반려동물 구조 단체의 인터넷 사이트에서도 찾아볼 수 있어.

후안: 알겠어. 그냥 선택만하면 그 반려견을 너한테 보내주는 거야?

웬디: 아니야, 입양서를 작성해야 하는데 단체에서 가정 점검을 하러 오는 것 같아.

후안: 와, 생각했던 것보다 훨씬 더 복잡하네.

웬디: 응, 내 생각에 개를 파양시키지 않을 좋은 집인지를 단체에서 확인하려고 하는 것 같아. 동물들이 입양되었다가 보호소로 다시 돌아오는 경우가 많다고 들었어.

후안: 음, 발리와 새로운 개가 사이좋게 지내길 바래.

웬디: 나도 그랬으면 해. 빨리 개를 입양하고 싶어!

ADOPTING A DOG

Wendy: I think Barley needs a buddy.

Juan: You want to get another dog? Are you sure you have time for that?

Wendy: Yeah, I think it's time.

Juan: Okay, what kind of dog are you thinking of getting?

Wendy: I'm not sure, but I know I want to adopt one. There are a lot of dogs at the shelter, so I want to adopt a rescue.

Juan: But aren't you worried about the dog's personality? What if the dog is mean?

Wendy: My friends have rescues and each dog is so loving. I think the dogs are grateful to be in a loving home and their loving personalities seem to reflect that.

Juan: I guess that's true. Your friend's dog Brisket seems to be very loving, and I know he was adopted.

Wendy: Exactly!

Juan: So where are you going to go to adopt a dog? The pound?

Wendy: Yeah, but I can also go on the Internet sites for adoption centers or pet rescue organizations to find one.

Juan: I see. Do you just pick one and they deliver the pet to you?

Wendy: No, you have to fill out an adoption form, and I think someone from the organization comes over to do a home check.

Juan: Wow, this is much more complicated than I thought.

Wendy: Yeah, I think they're just trying to make sure that the dog is going to a good home permanently. I have heard that many animals are returned to shelters after they are adopted.

Juan: Well, hopefully Barley and the new dog will get along.

Wendy: I hope so, too. I can't wait to adopt another dog!

69

해변에서의 하루

-

A DAY AT THE BEACH (B1)

조쉬: 안녕, 레베카! 네가 못 오나 보다 생각하려던 참이야. 네가 여기 와줘서 기뻐.

레베카: 응, 오는 데 시간이 좀 걸렸어. 해변에 좀 더 가깝게 살고 싶어서 캘리포니아로 이사했는데 그럴 만한 가치가 있어. 게다가, 요즘 날씨가 너무 좋아.

조쉬: 하지만 넌 웨스트 코비나에 살고 있잖아. 해변에서 네 시간 거리 아니야?

레베카: 맞아, 그런데 그건 교통 체증이 있을 때고, 오늘은 두 시간밖에 걸리지 않았어.

조쉬: 그래도 머네, 그건 그렇고! 배고파? 여기 음식이 엄청 많아.

레베카: 응! 뭐 있어?

조쉬: 일반 핫도그, 매운 핫도그, 베이컨으로 감싼 핫도그, 그리고 칠면조 핫도그가 있어.

레베카: 핫도그가 아닌 건 있어?

조쉬: 내 생각에 나다니엘이 마지막 햄버거를 먹은 것 같아. 하지만 감자칩이랑 소스도 많이 있고 저기 아이스박스 안에는 음료도 종류별로 있어.

레베카: 좋네! 사실, 베이컨으로 감싼 핫도그 남은 게 있다면 먹을래.

조쉬: 좋아, 여기 있어.

레베카: 고마워, 맛있게 생겼네! 근데 선크림 있어? 내 거는 집에 두고 온 것 같아.

조쉬: 응, 여기 조금 있어.

레베카: 고마워! 너도 같이 배구 하러 갈거야?

조쉬: 아마도, 근데 방금 음식을 먹었으니까 삼십 분 정도 기다렸다가 놀 거야. 배탈이 나고 싶지는 않거든.

레베카: 좋은 생각이야. 내 팀에 들어올래?

조쉬: 당연하지!

레베카: 좋아! 정말 재미있을 거야!

A DAY AT THE BEACH

Josh: Hey, Rebecca! I was beginning to think you weren't going make it. I'm glad you're here.

Rebecca: Yeah, it took a while to get here. I moved to California to be closer to the beach so this is worth it. Plus, the weather has been beautiful lately.

Josh: But you live in West Covina. Aren't you four hours from the beach?

Rebecca: Yeah, but that's with traffic. It only took me two hours today.

Josh: That's still pretty far, but all right! Hey, are you hungry? We have lots of food here.

Rebecca: I am! What do you have?

Josh: We have regular hot dogs, spicy hot dogs, bacon-wrapped hot dogs, and turkey hot dogs.

Rebecca: Do you have anything that's not a hot dog?

Josh: I think Nathaniel ate the last hamburger. But we have tons of chips and dip and all kinds of beverages in the coolers over there.

Rebecca: Great! Actually, I'll have a bacon-wrapped hot dog if you have any left.

Josh: Sure, here you go.

Rebecca: Thanks, this looks delicious! By the way, do you have any sunscreen? I think I left mine at the house.

Josh: Yes, I have some right here.

Rebecca: Thanks! Are you going to play volleyball with everyone?

Josh: Probably, but I just ate so I'm going to wait half an hour before I play. I don't want to get a stomachache.

Rebecca: Good idea. Do you want to be on my team?

Josh: Sure!

Rebecca: Great! This is going to be so much fun!

70

치즈버거를 만들자
-
LET'S MAKE CHEESEBURGERS (B1)

휘트니: 배고프다. 종일 굶었어.

존: 뭐 먹고 싶어? 나도 배고파.

휘트니: 치즈버거 먹고 싶어. 만드는 법 좀 가르쳐 줄래? 너 치즈버거 완전 맛있게 만들잖아!

존: 물론이지!

휘트니: 나한테 재료가 몇 가지 있어.

존: 정말? 햄버거 빵 있어?

휘트니: 응. 다진 소고기도 있어.

존: 양념은?

휘트니: 머스터드, 마요네즈, 케첩, 그리고 스위트 렐리쉬가 있어.

존: 완벽해! 네가 원하는 지는 모르겠지만, 나한테 양상추랑 토마토도 조금 있더라고.

휘트니: 나는 특제 소스와 미국식 치즈를 곁들인 버거를 먹을 거야.

존: 알았어, 좋아. 햄버거를 만들기 전에 재료를 전부 준비하자.

휘트니: 내가 뭘 할까?

존: 내가 빵을 굽는 동안 네가 특제 소스를 만들면 되겠다. 그릇에 머스터드, 마요네즈, 케첩, 스위트 렐리쉬를 같은 양으로 넣고 함께 섞으면 돼.

휘트니: 알았어.

존: 빵에 버터를 조금 발라서 구울게.

휘트니: 특제 소스는 준비됐어. 다음엔 뭘 하지?

존: 도마 위에 다진 소고기를 놓고 고르게 치댄 다음에 동그랗게 빚어.

휘트니: 중간에 노른자를 넣을까?

존: 응! 기억력 좋네! 올리브 오일도 조금 두르고 소금과 후추를 뿌려. 그런 다음, 모두 섞어서 다진 소고기를 두 개의 미트볼로 만들어. 고기를 너무 세게 다지지는 말고. 난 프라이팬을 준비할게.

휘트니: 다음은 뭐할까?

존: 달궈진 프라이팬에 미트볼을 놓고 납작하게 눌러. 패티를 앞뒤로 일 분씩 익혀. 그러고 나서 치즈를 위에 얹어. 마지막으로 불을 끄고 버거를 몇 분간 그대로 둬. 버거가 식으면 만들어 먹을 수 있어.

휘트니: 좋아! 너무 기대돼!

LET'S MAKE CHEESEBURGERS

Whitney: I'm hungry. I haven't eaten all day.

John: What do you want to eat? I am hungry, too.

Whitney: I want a cheeseburger. Can you show me how to make one? You make really good cheeseburgers!

John: Sure!

Whitney: I have some ingredients for us.

John: Really? Do you have hamburger buns?

Whitney: Yes. I also have ground beef.

John: What about condiments?

Whitney: I have mustard, mayonnaise, ketchup, and sweet relish.

John: Perfect! I happen to have some lettuce and tomatoes if you want some.

Whitney: I think I will have a burger with special sauce and American cheese.

John: Okay, cool. Let's get everything prepped before we make the burgers.

Whitney: What would you like me to do?

John: You can make the special sauce while I toast the buns. Mix equal parts mustard, mayonnaise, ketchup, and sweet relish together in a bowl.

Whitney: Okay.

John: I will toast the buns with a little bit of butter.

Whitney: The special sauce is ready. What do I do next?

John: Crumble the ground beef on a cutting board and make a circle with the ground beef.

Whitney: Do I add the egg yolk in the middle?

John: Yes! Good memory! You should also drizzle some olive oil and sprinkle on some salt and pepper. Then, mix everything together and form two balls from the ground beef. Don't pack the meat too tightly. I will get the pan ready.

Whitney: What do we do next?

John: Once the pan is hot, place a meat ball on the pan and then smash the ball into a patty. Cook the patty for a minute on each side. Then, add the cheese on top. Finally, turn off the heat and let the burger rest for a few minutes. Once the burger is cool, you can make your burger and eat it.

Whitney: Sounds great! I can't wait!

71

음식에 머리카락이 있어
-
THERE'S A HAIR IN MY FOOD (B1)

제럴드: 샐러드 어때?

밀리: 괜찮아. 그렇게 맛있진 않고. 네 팟파이는 어때?

제럴드: 사실, 맛있어. 맛이 아주 다양해. 그리고... 맙소사. 이상한 것도 있어.

밀리: 뭔데?

제럴드: 머리카락.

밀리: 머리카락? 사람 머리카락?

제럴드: 응, 그리고 꽤 길어.

밀리: 확실해?

제럴드: 바로 여기 있어.

밀리: 제럴드...

제럴드: 아니, 여기 레스토랑 싸지 않잖아. 음식에 머리카락이 있으면 안 되지.

밀리: 제럴드!

제럴드: 왜?

밀리: 네 팟파이에 있는 머리카락이 하얀색이야.

제럴드: 그래서? 말하려는 게 뭐야?

밀리: 주위를 둘러봐. 여기 흰머리를 가진 사람은 아무도 없어.

제럴드: 아...

밀리: 네 머리카락인 것 같아.

THERE'S A HAIR IN MY FOOD

Gerald: How's your salad?

Millie: It's okay. Not amazing. How's your potpie?

Gerald: It's great, actually. It has a ton of flavor. And... oh my gosh. It has something else, too.

Millie: What?

Gerald: A hair.

Millie: A hair? A human hair?

Gerald: Yeah, and it's pretty long.

Millie: Are you sure?

Gerald: It's right here.

Millie: Gerald...

Gerald: I mean, this restaurant isn't cheap. There shouldn't be hair in our food.

Millie: Gerald!

Gerald: What is it?

Millie: The hair in your potpie is white.

Gerald: So? What's your point?

Millie: Take a look around. There's no one else here who has white hair.

Gerald: Uh...

Millie: I think that's your hair.

72

오른손잡이 아니면 왼손잡이?

-

RIGHT-HANDED OR LEFT-HANDED? (B1)

산티아고: 로렌 씨 오른손잡이죠, 그렇죠?

로렌: 네. 산티아고 씨도 그렇죠?

산티아고: 네. 하지만 제 아버지와 형은 왼손잡이예요.

로렌: 아, 재미있네요. 오른손잡이와 왼손잡이는 유전일까요?

산티아고: 모르겠어요. 주로 사용하는 손이 성격이랑 그 밖의 특징들과 연관이 있다고 듣긴 했어요.

로렌: 정말요? 어떤 얘기를 들었나요?

산티아고: 사실인지는 모르겠지만, 오른손잡이가 지능 테스트에서 점수를 높게 받고 장수한다고 읽었어요.

로렌: 와. 말도 안 돼요.

산티아고: 그리고 왼손잡이가 좀 더 창의적이고 더 천재적인 경향이 있어요. 아, 왼손잡이는 오른손잡이보다 이십오 퍼센트 정도 돈을 더 많이 벌어요.

로렌: 우와. 왜 그런지 궁금해요.

산티아고: 글쎄요, 제가 왼손잡이였다면 천재가 되어 그 이유를 이해했을지도 몰라요!

로렌: 하하, 맞아요! 그걸 이해할 만큼 똑똑하지는 않네요.

산티아고: 왼손잡이였던 세계적인 지도자와 역사적인 인물들도 많아요. 오바마가 왼손잡이예요. 또 조지 부시와 빌 클린턴도 그렇고요. 아마도 알렉산더 대왕, 율리우스 카이사르, 나폴레옹도 왼손잡이었던 것 같아요. 그리고 커트 코베인과 지미 헨드릭스 같은 음악가도 있어요.

로렌: 와, 어떻게 여기에 대해 그렇게 많이 아세요?

산티아고: 모르겠네요! 흥미로운 것 같아요.

로렌: 맞아요. 이제 제가 왼손잡이였으면 좋겠네요.

산티아고: 글쎄요, 로렌 씨가 스물여덟 살인데 지금 그걸 바꿀 수 있을지는 모르겠네요!

RIGHT-HANDED OR LEFT-HANDED?

Santiago: You're right-handed, aren't you?

Lauren: Yeah. You are too, right?

Santiago: Yes. But my dad and brother are left-handed.

Lauren: Oh, interesting. Does right- and left-handedness run in families?

Santiago: I have no idea. But I've heard that personality and other characteristics are connected to your dominant hand.

Lauren: Really? What have you heard?

Santiago: I'm not sure if it's true, but I read that right-handed people often score higher on intelligence tests and they live longer.

Lauren: Oh wow. No way.

Santiago: And left-handed people tend to be more creative and are more likely to be geniuses. Oh, and left-handed people earn something like 25 percent more money than right-handed people.

Lauren: Whoa. I wonder why that happens.

Santiago: Well, maybe if I were left-handed I'd be a genius and understand why!

Lauren: Ha ha, true! We aren't smart enough to understand it.

Santiago: There have also been a lot of world leaders and historical figures who were left-handed. Obama is left-handed. So are George W. Bush and Bill Clinton. Supposedly, Alexander the Great, Julius Caesar, and Napoleon were lefties. And some musicians like Kurt Cobain and Jimi Hendrix.

Lauren: Wow, how do you know so much about this?

Santiago: I don't know! I think it's fascinating.

Lauren: It is. Now I wish I were left-handed.

Santiago: Well, you're twenty-eight years old, so I'm not sure you can change that now!

73

병 속의 메시지
-
MESSAGE IN A BOTTLE (B1)

스콧: 난 이 해변이 정말 좋아. 항상 사람이 없고 물도 참 맑아.

스카이: 우리를 위한 천국 같아.

스콧: 모래가 너무 부드러워! 가루 같아.

스카이: 흰 모래사장이 참 멋져.

스콧: 여기 정말 마음에 들지 않니?

스카이: 마음에 들어. 바다 바람은 정말 잔잔하면서 편안해. 우리 어서 수영하러 가야 해.

스콧: 맞아. 물이 정말 좋더라고!

스카이: 기다려봐... 저거 보여?

스콧: 뭘 봐?

스카이: 물 속에 반짝이는 무언가가 떠다녀. 병... 같이 생겼어.

스콧: 병 속에 쪽지가 있으면 재밌을 것 같지 않아?

스카이: 맞아, 재밌겠다!

스콧: 여기에 병이 있어. 코르크 마개가 있네.

스카이: 봐! 안에 무언가 말아져 있어. 종이 같아.

스콧: 잠깐만. 아하! 알았어.

스카이: 뭐라고 하는 거야?

스콧: 모르겠어... 글씨가 정말 오래되어서 알아보기가 어려워. 내가 보기에 뭐라고 써져 있냐면...

스카이: ...응?

스콧: 아니야. 아무것도 아니야.

스카이: 어서! 뭐라고 쓰여져 있는데? 나 정말 궁금해!

스콧: "어서 도망쳐..."라고 적혀 있어.

스카이: 하하. 너무 재미있다. 진짜 뭐라고 적혀 있는데?

스콧: 직접 봐.

스카이: 정말로 그렇게 적혀 있네. 엉뚱한 메시지야.

스콧: 응, 그런 것 같아.

스카이: 야, 멀리서 배가 보여. 근처에 배가 있을 거라고는 생각 못 했는데..

스콧: 쌍안경 가져 왔어?

스카이: 응, 여기 있어.

스콧: 고마워. 보자... 하얀 해골이랑 뼈 두 개가 "X"자 모양으로 그려져 있는 검정 깃발이 보여. 그리고 배가 이쪽으로 오고 있어.

스카이: 해적 같아!

스콧: 여기서 나가야 해. 뛰어!

MESSAGE IN A BOTTLE

Scott: I really love this beach. It's always empty and the water is so clear.

Sky: It's like our own little slice of heaven.

Scott: The sand is so soft! It feels like powder.

Sky: White sand beaches are so nice.

Scott: Don't you love this place?

Sky: I really do. The ocean breeze is so calming and relaxing. We should go for a swim soon.

Scott: I agree. The water feels great!

Sky: Wait... do you see that?

Scott: See what?

Sky: There's something shiny floating in the water. It looks like... a bottle.

Scott: Wouldn't it be funny if there was a message in that bottle?

Sky: Yeah, that'd be funny!

Scott: Here's the bottle. It has a cork.

Sky: And look! I think there's something rolled up inside. Looks like paper.

Scott: Give me a second. Aha! Got it.

Sky: What does it say?

Scott: I don't know... it's hard to make out because the writing looks really old. From what I can tell, I think it says...

Sky: ...Well?

Scott: Nothing. It's nothing.

Sky: Come on! What does it say? I'm so curious!

Scott: It says, "Run for your lives..."

Sky: Ha ha. Very funny. What does it actually say?

Scott: See for yourself.

Sky: It... really does say that. What a silly message.

Scott: Yeah, I guess.

Sky: Hey, I see a ship in the distance. I didn't think there would be any ships nearby.

Scott: Did you bring the binoculars?

Sky: Yeah, here they are.

Scott: Thanks. I see... a black flag with a white skull and two bones in an "X" shape. And the ship is coming this way.

Sky: I think those are pirates!

Scott: We have to get out of here. Run!

74

거기에 어떻게 가는거야?

-

HOW DO I GET THERE? (B1)

제프리: 너의 새집을 보게 되다니 너무 신나!

사리나: 야호, 나도!

제프리: 네가 이사한 이후로 내가 네 새집에 가보지 않았다는 게 믿어지지가 않아.

사리나: 괜찮아! 네가 그동안 너무 바빴어.

제프리: 응, 맞아. 일이 좀 널널해져서 다행이야. 삼 개월 정도 사교 활동을 못했어!

사리나: 음, 넌 이제 막 사업을 시작했잖아. 일이 그렇게 바쁜 건 이해할 만해.

제프리: 많이 바쁠 거라는 걸 알았지만 내가 생각했던 것보다 훨씬 더 심했어. 그래도 나 자신을 위해 일하는 게 너무 좋아. 스트레스는 받지만 결국에는 모든 게 가치가 있어.

사리나: 그 말을 들으니 기쁘네.

제프리: 그럼, 너희 집에 갈 때 그냥 휴대폰에 지도 앱을 사용해서 가면 돼?

사리나: 내가 길을 알려 줄게. 사람들이 여기서 길을 잘 잃었거든.

제프리: 알았어. 어떻게 가야 해?

사리나: 구십사 이스트를 타고 스프링 스트릿으로 가. 그리고 고속도로를 나가서 우회전을 해. 오른쪽으로 꺾자마자 바로 오른쪽으로 또 꺾어. 거기가 길이 좁아서 사람들이 많이 놓쳐.

제프리: 그러니까 고속도로 나와서 우회전하라는 거지. 그리고 좁은 길에서 바로 우회전을 다시 하고.

사리나: 맞아. 그 다음에는 두 블록 정도 직진하고 오크 트리

레인에서 좌회전을 해. 언덕을 올라가. 언덕 꼭대기에서 우회전을 해. 앞에 야자수가 있는 하얀색 집이 우리 집이야.

제프리: 응, 알았어. 고마워! 여섯 시 삼십 분쯤 도착할 거야. 길을 잃으면 알려 줄게.

사리나: 응, 길 안내가 더 필요하면 전화해! 좋아, 곧 봐!

제프리: 곧 보자!

HOW DO I GET THERE?

Jeffrey: I'm so excited to see your new place!

Sarina: Yay, me too!

Jeffrey: I can't believe I haven't visited you at your new house since you moved.

Sarina: It's okay! You've been so busy.

Jeffrey: Yeah, I have. I'm glad work has slowed down a bit. I haven't had a social life for, like, three months!

Sarina: Well, you just started a business. It's understandable that things have been so crazy.

Jeffrey: I knew it would be crazy, but it was even worse than I imagined! But I love working for myself. It's stressful but, in the end, all the work is worth it.

Sarina: That's great to hear.

Jeffrey: So, can I just use a maps app on my phone to get to your place?

Sarina: Actually, I'm going to give you directions. Some people have gotten lost on the way here.

Jeffrey: Okay, okay. So how do I get there?

Sarina: Take 94 East to Spring Street. Then turn right after you exit the freeway. Immediately after you turn right, turn right again. It's a small street and many people miss it.

Jeffrey: So, turn right after the freeway. Then make an immediate right again on a small street.

Sarina: Yes. And then go straight for about two blocks, and then turn left on Oak Tree Lane. Go up the hill. Turn right at the top of the hill. Our house is the white one with the palm tree in the front.

Jeffrey: Okay, got it. Thanks! I'll be there around 6:30. I'll let you know if I get lost.

Sarina: Yes, give me a call if you need more directions! All right, see you soon!

Jeffrey: See ya!

75

비행기 표 사기

-

BUYING A PLANE TICKET (B1)

팸: 나랑 같이 여행 갈래?

짐: 그럼! 뭐 생각해 둔 곳 있어?

팸: 피자가 정말 먹고 싶어, 그러니 뉴욕에 가자!

짐: 단지 피자 때문에 뉴욕까지 가고 싶다고??

팸: 응! 게다가 내 사촌을 방문할 거야. 본지 오래됐거든.

짐: 알았어, 그렇게 하자. 언제 가는 거야?

팸: 몇 주 후에 휴가를 사용할 수 있을 것 같아.

짐: 좋네. 나도 한 달 더 학교에 가지 않으니까.

팸: 온라인에서 비행기 표를 찾아보자. 지금 일부 항공사가 세일 하는 것 같은데 좋은 가격을 찾을 수 있으면 좋겠어.

짐: 저녁 시간에 맞춰서 거기에 도착할 수 있도록 아침 시간에 떠나는 게 좋을 것 같아.

팸: 도착하자마자 피자 먹어? 난 벌써 이 여행이 너무 좋아!

짐: 나도. 뭐 찾은 거 있어?

팸: 응, 지금 가장 싼 표가 한 사람당 왕복 이백팔십 달러인데, 야간 비행이야.

짐: 아침 비행은?

팸: 아... 칠백 달러나 해.

짐: 뭐라고?! 말도 안 돼!

팸: 맞지? 나는 야간 비행편은 보통 안 사는데 이건 가격 차이가 너무 크네.

짐: 맞아. 야간 비행을 사고 거기에 도착하자마자 낮잠을 자자.

팸: 알았어. 우리 마일리지 포인트 남은 거 있어?

짐: 없어, 근데 호텔 크레딧은 아직 남아 있어.

팸: 앗싸! 알겠어. 내 신용 카드로 방금 표 두 장을 샀어. 호텔은 네가 예약할 수 있어?

짐: 방금 했어. 우리 뉴욕에 가나 봐.

팸: 피자 먹으로 간다!

BUYING A PLANE TICKET

Pam: Would you like to go on a trip with me?

Jim: Sure! What do you have in mind?

Pam: I really want some pizza, so we're going to New York!

Jim: You want to go all the way to New York just for pizza?

Pam: Yes! Plus, we'll get to visit my cousins. I haven't seen them in ages.

Jim: Okay, let's do it. When are we going?

Pam: I think I will be able to use some vacation time in a few weeks.

Jim: That's good because I don't start school for another month.

Pam: Let's check online for some plane tickets. I think some of the airlines are having a sale right now, so hopefully we can get some great deals.

Jim: We should probably try to leave in the morning so we can get there in time for dinner.

Pam: Pizza as soon as we land? I am loving this journey already!

Jim: Me too. Have you found anything?

Pam: Yeah, the lowest ticket price right now is $280 round trip per person, but it's a red-eye flight.

Jim: What about the morning flights?

Pam: Uh... $700.

Jim: What?! That's ridiculous!

Pam: Right? I normally don't purchase overnight flights, but the price difference is too great.

Jim: I agree. Let's buy the red-eye flight tickets and take a nap as soon as we get there.

Pam: Okay. Do we have any mileage points left?

Jim: No, but we still have hotel credit leftover.

Pam: Yay! All right, I just purchased two tickets with my credit card. Can you book us a hotel?

Jim: Just did. I guess we're going to New York.

Pam: Pizza, here we come!

76

집 청소하기

-

CLEANING THE HOUSE (B1)

트레이시: 청소하는 날이야!

랜던: 한 달 중 내가 가장 좋아하는 날이지!

트레이시: 하하. 어떤 방을 할래?

랜던: 음, 부엌 빼고 아무데나 할게.

트레이시: 알았어, 좋아. 네가 화장실을 하면 내가 부엌을 할게.

랜던: 좋아.

트레이시: 그리고 내가 침실을 할게. 넌 거실 할래?

랜던: 응. 차고지는 어떻게 해?

트레이시: 아, 거긴 다음에 하자. 차고지 청소하는 데만 하루 종일 걸릴 거야.

랜던: 맞아. 청소용품은 다 싱크대 밑에 있어?

트레이시: 응 그리고 네가 필요하다면 식기실에 여분의 키친 타월도 있어.

랜던: 좋아. 청소 음악을 틀을 게!

트레이시: 하하. 그게 어떤 종류의 음악이야?

랜던: 오늘은 팔십 년대 록을 틀거야. 난 청소하는게 너무 싫으니 동기 부여가 필요해!

트레이시: 네가 좋다면 뭐든 좋아!

랜던: *(화장실 청소 중)* 자기야, 왜 이렇게 샴푸가 많이 필요해?

트레이시: 난 샴푸 그렇게 많이 안 갖고 있는데..

랜던: 여기 네 샴푸 다른 종류로 네 가지나 있잖아.

트레이시: 글쎄, 다른 종류를 써보고 내가 제일 좋아하는 게 어떤 건지 알고 싶어.

랜던: 그냥 샴푸일 뿐이야!

트레이시: 내 머리카락은 중요해! 자기는 왜 같은 운동화를 다른 색으로 세 켤레나 갖고 있어?

랜던: 난 운동화를 좋아해!

트레이시: 어머, 이 키친 타월 버려야 할까? 많이 찢어졌어.

랜던: 응, 버려도 될 거야.

트레이시: 알았어, 부엌은 끝났어. 침실을 청소할 시간이야!

랜던: 알았어!

CLEANING THE HOUSE

Tracy: It's cleaning day!

Landon: My favorite day of the month!

Tracy: Ha ha. Which rooms do you want to tackle?

Landon: Umm, I'll do anything except the kitchen.

Tracy: Okay, fine. I'll do the kitchen if you do the bathroom.

Landon: That works.

Tracy: And I'll do the bedroom. Do you want to do the living room?

Landon: Sure. What about the garage?

Tracy: Ugh. Let's just save that for next time. That'll take a whole day by itself.

Landon: True. Are all the cleaning products under the sink?

Tracy: Yeah and there are extra paper towels in the pantry if you need them.

Landon: Cool. I'm going to put on some cleaning music!

Tracy: Ha ha. What kind of music is that?

Landon: Today it's 80s rock. I hate cleaning, so I need to stay motivated!

Tracy: Whatever works for you!

Landon: *(cleaning the bathroom)* Honey, why do you need so many shampoos?

Tracy: I don't have that many shampoos...

Landon: You have four different kinds here.

Tracy: Well, I like to try different types and see which one I like best.

Landon: It's just shampoo!

Tracy: My hair is important! Why do you have the same pair of sneakers in three different colors?

Landon: I like sneakers!

Tracy: Hey, should we throw out this kitchen towel? It's pretty torn up.

Landon: Yeah, we can probably get rid of it.

Tracy: All right, I'm done with the kitchen. Time to move on to the bedroom!

Landon: Okay!

77

개 아니면 고양이?

-

DOG OR CAT? (B1)

말리: 스디브! 나링 놀래? 나 지금 너무 심심해!

스티브: 안 돼, 말리. 오늘은 그럴 시간이 없어.

말리: 에이, 게임 하자! 재밌을 거야!

스티브: 안 돼.

말리: 라자냐 가져왔는데!

스티브: ...좋아. 라자냐 이리 줘봐.

말리: 게임 하고 나서 네가 원하는 라자냐를 다 먹을 수 있어!

스티브: 알았어, 무슨 게임인데?

말리: 개와 고양이 중에 어떤 것이 나은가?

스티브: 이 게임은 어떻게 하는거야?

말리: 내가 개가 더 나은 이유를 나열하면 너는 고양이가 더 나은 이유를 나열해야만 해.

스티브: 그러고 나서?

말리: 그러고 나서 더 나은 이유를 생각해 내는 사람이 승자야.

스티브: 누가 승자를 결정해?

말리: 우리 둘 다!

스티브: 말이 안 되지만 라자냐가 너무 맛있게 생겼어.

말리: 네가 먹을 최고의 라자냐야!

스티브: 알았어, 좋아. 너의 바보 같은 게임을 할게.

말리: 좋았어! 내가 먼저 할게.

스티브: 시작해.

말리: 알았어, 개들은 대단해. 왜냐하면, 그들은 사랑스럽고, 충성스럽고, 장난치기 좋아하고, 아주 재미있고, 웃기고, 바보 같고, 푹신하고, 빠르고, 똑똑하고, 정말로, 정말로 재미있고, 정말로, 정말로 장난치기 좋아하고, 그리고 던진 물건을 물어올 수 있고, 정말로 빨리 달리고, 정말로 시끄럽게 짖기 때문이야! 아, 그리고 최고의 후각을 가졌어!

스티브: 몇 개는 이미 했던 말이야.

말리: 아니야, 아주 재미있고랑 정말 정말 재미있고는 달라. 이제 네 차례야!

스티브: 안 할래.

말리: 뭐라고?

스티브: 그럴 가치가 없어.

말리: 아, 어서!

스티브: 나중에 봐, 말리.

DOG OR CAT?

Marley: Steve! Do you want to play? I'm so bored right now!

Steve: No, Marley. I don't have time for this today.

Marley: Come on, let's play a game! It'll be fun!

Steve: No.

Marley: But I've brought lasagna!

Steve: ...fine. Hand over the lasagna.

Marley: You can have all the lasagna you want after we play a game!

Steve: All right, what's the game?

Marley: Which is better: dog or cat?

Steve: How do we play this game?

Marley: I'll list reasons why dogs are better and you have to list reasons why cats are better.

Steve: And then?

Marley: And then the winner is whoever comes up with better reasons.

Steve: Who decides on the winner?

Marley: We both do!

Steve: This doesn't make sense, but that lasagna looks really good.

Marley: It's the best lasagna you will ever have!

Steve: Okay, fine. I'll play your silly game.

Marley: Great! I'll go first.

Steve: Go on.

Marley: Okay, so dogs are great because they are loving, loyal, playful, super fun, funny, silly, fluffy, fast, smart, really, really fun, really, really playful, and they can play fetch, run really fast, and bark really loud! Oh, and they have the best sense of smell!

Steve: Some of those were repeated.

Marley: No, super fun is different from really, really fun. Now it's your turn!

Steve: No.

Marley: What?

Steve: This isn't worth it.

Marley: Oh, come on!

Steve: See you later, Marley.

78

커피숍 방문

-

VISITING A COFFEE SHOP (B1)

라일리: 안녕하세요, 환영합니다! 주문하시겠어요?

누르: 안녕하세요. 음... 커피를 마시고 싶은데 오늘은 어떤 걸 마실지 모르겠어요.

라일리: 글쎄요, 드립 커피와 라떼나 카푸치노와 같은 에스프레소 음료도 있고요. 아니면 푸어오버와 같이 무언가 색다른 것을 원하시나요?

누르: 푸어오버가 무엇인가요? 커피숍들 메뉴에서 계속 보이는데 뭔지 모르겠어요.

라일리: 푸어오버 커피는 여기 계산대에서 보이는 도구와 용기로 만들어집니다. 갓 갈아 놓은 커피에 바리스타가 천천히 뜨거운 물을 부으면 커피가 이 깔때기 모양의 용기로 추출됩니다.

누르: 아, 알겠어요! 설명해줘서 감사합니다.

라일리: 별 말씀을요. 천천히 시간을 갖고 주문할 준비가 되시면 제게 알려주세요.

누르: 준비된 것 같아요. 미디움 사이즈로 바닐라 라떼 한 잔 주시겠어요?

라일리: 알겠습니다. 우유는 어떤 걸로 하시겠어요?

누르: 아몬드 우유로 부탁합니다.

라일리: 좋아요. 드실 거는 필요 없으신가요?

누르: 음, 오렌지 스콘을 먹을게요.

라일리: 제가 좋아하는 거예요.

누르: 그래요? 맛있어 보여요!

라일리: 맛있어요! 미디움 사이즈 바닐라 라떼와 오렌지 스콘 주문하셔서 총 육 달러 칠십팔 센트입니다.

누르: 좋아요. 여기 제 카드입니다.

라일리: 여기에 그냥 카드를 넣으시면 됩니다.

누르: 아, 그렇군요.

라일리: 좋아요, 다 됐습니다! 좋은 하루 보내세요!

누르: 감사합니다. 좋은 하루 보내세요!

VISITING A COFFEE SHOP

Riley: Hi, welcome! What can I get for you?

Nour: Hi. Can I get a.... hmm... I want coffee but I'm not sure what kind today.

Riley: Well, are you in the mood for drip coffee? An espresso drink like a latte or cappuccino? Or something different like a pour over?

Nour: What's a pour over? I keep seeing that on coffee shop menus and I don't know what it is.

Riley: A pour over coffee is made with the tools and containers you see on the counter here. The barista slowly pours hot water over freshly ground coffee and the coffee comes out in this funnel-shaped container.

Nour: Ah, I see! Thanks for that explanation.

Riley: No problem. Take your time and let me know when you're ready to order.

Nour: I think I'm ready. Can I have a medium vanilla latte?

Riley: Sure. What kind of milk would you like in that?

Nour: Almond milk, please.

Riley: No problem. Would you like anything to eat?

Nour: Umm, sure. I'll have an orange scone.

Riley: Those are my favorite.

Nour: Yeah? It looks good!

Riley: It is! Okay, so with the medium vanilla latte and orange scone your total comes to $6.78.

Nour: Great. Here's my card.

Riley: Actually, you can just insert it here.

Nour: Oh, I see.

Riley: Okay, you're all set! Have a good day!

Nour: Thanks. You too!

79

내 열쇠를 못 찾겠어
-
I CAN'T FIND MY KEYS (B1)

리나: 대니, 내 열쇠 봤어?

대니: 문 옆에 있는 탁자 위에 없어?

리나: 없어.

대니: 부엌 조리대는 확인해 봤어?

리나: 전부 살펴봤어.

대니: 침실까지? 화장실은?

리나: 응, 침실이랑 화장실도 살펴봤지. 두 번씩이나.

대니: 열쇠를 마지막으로 본 장소가 어디야?

리나: 열쇠를 가지고 집안을 걸어 다녔던 건 기억해. 그게 마지막이야.

대니: 너한테 이런 일이 항상 일어나!

리나: 알고 있어. 난 정리를 좀 해야 해.

대니: 열쇠를 늘 같은 장소에 보관해야 해. 그렇게 하면 열쇠를 잃어버리지 않을 거야.

리나: 응, 네 말이 맞아. 하지만 지금은 열쇠를 찾아야 해.

대니: 알았어, 내가 열쇠를 찾는 걸 도와줄게. 내가 거실을 살펴볼 테니까. 너는 침실과 화장실을 다시 한 번 살펴봐. 네 생각에 차 안에 열쇠를 뒀을 것 같진 않아?

리나: 안 뒀지, 차 문을 잠그고 집에 들어 갔으니까.

대니: 좋은 지적이야.

리나: 침대 위에 없고. 침대 밑에도 없어. 땅바닥에도 없어. 세면대나 화장실 서랍에도 없어.

대니: 가방 안에는 확인해 봤어?

리나: 당연히 해봤지!

대니: 다시 한 번 확인해 봐, 혹시 모르니까.

리나: .....

대니: 뭐야?

리나: 열쇠를 찾았어.

대니: 어디서?

리나: 내 가방에서.

대니: 맙소사...

I CAN'T FIND MY KEYS

Li Na: Danny, have you seen my keys?

Danny: They're not on the table by the door?

Li Na: No.

Danny: Have you checked the kitchen counter?

Li Na: I've looked everywhere.

Danny: Even the bedroom? What about the bathroom?

Li Na: Yes, I've looked in the bedroom and the bathroom. Twice.

Danny: Where was the last place you saw them?

Li Na: I remember walking in the house with them. And that's the last time I remember seeing them.

Danny: This always happens to you!

Li Na: I know. I need to get more organized!

Danny: You should put them back in the same place every time. That way you won't lose them.

Li Na: Yeah, you're right. But right now I just need to find them.

Danny: Okay, I'll help you search for them. I'll look in the living room, and you can look again in the bedroom and bathroom. Do you think you could have left them in your car?

Li Na: No, because I had to lock my car and then get into the house.

Danny: Good point.

Li Na: They're not on the bed. They're not under the bed. They're not on the ground. They're not on the bathroom counter or in the bathroom drawers.

Danny: Did you check your purse?

Li Na: Of course I did!

Danny: Maybe check again, just in case.

Li Na: .....

Danny: What?

Li Na: I found them.

Danny: Where?

Li Na: In my purse.

Danny: Oh my gosh…

80

비가 와!

-

IT'S RAINING! (B1)

아키라: 내 생각에 오늘은 비가 올 것 같아.

야시르: 정말? 일기 예보에서 맑을 거라고 했는데.

아키라: 내가 본 예보는 비가 올 확률이 삼십 퍼센트라고 했어.

야시르: 확실해? 우리가 사는 도시를 찾아본 게 맞아?

아키라: 응, 그런 것 같아! 그냥 휴대폰에 있는 날씨 앱에서 봤어.

야시르: 이상하네.

아키라: 혹시 모르니까 우산 가져가.

야시르: 싫어.

아키라: 알았어! 내가 너한테 알려주지 않았다고 말하지나 마!

야시르: 하하. 알았어!

(여덟 시간 후...)

아키라: 일은 어땠어?

야시르: 좋았는데 바빴어. 지금 조깅을 하러 갈 거야.

아키라: 서둘러야 해! 구름이 심상치 않아.

야시르: 비는 안 올거야, 아키라!

아키라: 흠, 두고 보자고.

(이십 분 후에 야시르가 돌아왔다)

아키라: 맙소사, 흠뻑 젖었네!

야시르: 달리는 데 비가 오기 시작하더라고!

아키라: 비가 올 거라고 했잖아!

야시르: 으윽, 알겠어, 네가 옳았어. 네 말을 들었어야만 했는데.

아키라: 봤지? 나는 항상 옳아.

야시르: 항상은 아니지만... 자주 옳지.

아키라: 하하, 고마워! 이제 가서 옷이나 갈아입어!

IT'S RAINING!

Akira: I think it's going to rain today.

Yasir: Really? The weather forecast said it would be sunny.

Akira: The forecast I saw said there was a 30 percent chance of rain.

Yasir: Are you sure? Were you looking at the right city?

Akira: Uh, I think so! I was just looking at the weather app on my phone.

Yasir: That's weird.

Akira: You should take an umbrella just in case.

Yasir: Nah.

Akira: All right! Don't say I didn't warn you!

Yasir: Ha ha. Okay!

(Eight hours later...)

Akira: How was work?

Yasir: It was good but busy. I'm going to go for a run now.

Akira: You should hurry! The clouds look ominous.

Yasir: It's not going to rain, Akira!

Akira: Hmm, we'll see.

(Yasir returns twenty minutes later.)

Akira: Oh my gosh, you're soaked!

Yasir: It started raining while I was running!

Akira: I told you it was going to rain!

Yasir: Ugh, fine, you were right. I should have listened to you.

Akira: See? I'm always right.

Yasir: Not always, but... a lot of the time.

Akira: Ha ha, thanks! Now go get into some dry clothes!

81

미안합니다
-
I'M SORRY (B1)

매트: 다나에게 사과하고 싶어요. 제가 다나에게 무례했던 것에 대해서 기분이 좋지 않아요.

베스: 좋은 생각인 것 같아요.

매트: 어떻게 사과해야 할까요?

베스: 전화해서 만나자고 물어봐요. 무슨 일이 있었는지 말해주고 사과하고 싶다고 다나에게 말해 보세요.

매트: 알겠어요, 다나에게 방금 전화했어요. 다음 주에 만날 거예요.

베스: 좋네요. 다나 씨가 매트 씨를 만나겠다고 하니 제가 기쁘네요.

매트: 저도요. 그럼, 만나서 뭐라고 얘기해야 할까요?

베스: 미안하다고 하고 왜 미안한지도 말해야 좋아요. 그리고 다나 씨 기분이 어떤지도 물어보시고요.

매트: 맞아요. 저는 후회할 말을 하는 게 정말 싫어요. 가끔 그냥 제 입을 닫을 수 있으면 좋겠어요.

베스: 사람들은 모두 후회할 일을 해요. 다행인 것은 매트 씨의 잘못을 알고 거기에 대해 사과를 하고 싶어 한다는 거죠. 모두가 그렇지는 않거든요.

매트: 그런가봐요. 다나와 저는 오랫동안 친구였어요. 제가 다나를 처음 만났을 때를 기억해요. 저희 둘 다 대학에서 공룡에 관한 수업을 듣고 있었어요.

베스: 공룡이요?!

매트: 네, 멋졌어요! 어느 날 수업 중에 우리가 서로 나란히 앉아서 이야기를 시작했어요. 그러더니 어느샌가 우리가 거의 매일 함께 놀고 있더라고요!

베스: 오, 너무 멋지네요. 틀림없이 다나 씨가 매트 씨를 용서해줄 거예요. 너무 걱정하지 않아도 돼요.

매트: 베스 씨 말이 맞기를 바래요. 다나와의 우정은 제게 정말 중요해요.

베스: 다나 씨도 그건 알고 있을 거예요. 다음 주에 행운을 빌어요! 어떻게 되어 가는지 알려 주세요.

매트: 그럴게요.

I'M SORRY

Matt: I want to apologize to Dana. I was rude to her and I feel bad about it.

Beth: I think that's a good idea.

Matt: How should I apologize?

Beth: You should call her and ask her to meet you. Tell her you want to talk about what happened and apologize.

Matt: Okay, I just called her. We're going to meet next week.

Beth: That's good. I'm happy she agreed to meet with you.

Matt: Me too. So, what do I say when I see her?

Beth: You should tell her you're sorry and why you're sorry. And make sure she tells you how she feels too.

Matt: Yeah. I hate it when I say something that I regret. I wish I could just keep my mouth shut sometimes.

Beth: Everyone does things they regret. The good thing is that you realized what you said was wrong and you want to apologize for it. Not everyone would do that.

Matt: I guess. Dana and I have been friends for so many years. I remember when I first met her. We were both taking a class on dinosaurs in college.

Beth: Dinosaurs?!

Matt: Yeah, it was cool! We sat next to each other in class one day and we just started talking. And then before I knew it, we were hanging out almost every day!

Beth: Aww, that's so nice. I'm sure she'll forgive you. I wouldn't worry too much.

Matt: I hope you're right. Her friendship is really important to me.

Beth: I think she understands that. Good luck next week! Let me know how it goes.

Matt: Will do.

82

베이비 샤워

-

A BABY SHOWER (B1)

카일: 뭐 하고 있어요?

제나: 애니의 베이비 샤워를 위해서 파티 선물을 만들고 있어요!

카일: 어떤 종류의 파티 선물인데요?

제나: 선크림, 선글라스, 쪼리, 그리고 해변에서 쓸 수 있는 재미있는 것들로 채워진 비치백이에요. 손님들은 각각 자신의 이름이 적힌 가방을 받을 거예요.

카일: 좋은 생각이네요! 그리고 멋있어 보여요.

제나: 고마워요. 할 일이 엄청 많아요!

카일: 네, 하지만 애니가 정말로 행복해 할 거예요.

제나: 그러길 바래요!

카일: 그럼 베이비 샤워에서는 뭘 해요? 전 한 번도 가 본 적이 없어요.

제나: 베이비 샤워에 따라 다르다고 생각하지만 대게 자매나 친한 친구와 같이 예비 엄마와 가까운 사람이 파티를 계획해요. 음식을 먹고 게임도 하고, 가끔 예비 엄마가 선물을 열어 보기도 해요.

카일: 어떤 종류의 게임을 해요?

제나: 여러 가지 게임이 많아요. 인기가 많은 한 게임은 파티에서 "아기"라는 단어를 말할 수 없도록 하는 거예요. 손님들이 도착하면 기저귀 핀을 받고 각자 셔츠에 핀을 달아요. 만약 어떤 손님이 "아기"라고 말하는 것을 들었다면, 그 사람의 핀을 가져올 수 있어요. 가장 많은 핀을 가진 사람이 게임에서 이기는 거죠.

카일: 재미있네요.

제나: 네. 더러운 기저귀 같은 게임도 있어요.

카일: 음, 네?

제나: 하하. 실제로 "더러운" 기저귀를 쓰는 것은 아니에요. 녹인 초콜릿 바를 기저귀 안에 넣고 사람들이 그 기저귀를 돌려 가면서 어떤 종류의 초콜릿 바인지 맞추는 거예요.

카일: 와. 그건... 흥미롭네요.

제나: 네. 근데 재미있어요!

카일: 그럼, 파티에서 재미있게 놀기를 바랄게요! 그리고 모두가 틀림없이 비치백을 좋아할 거예요.

제나: 고마워요!

A BABY SHOWER

Kyle: What are you doing?

Jenna: I'm making party favors for Annie's baby shower!

Kyle: What kind of party favors?

Jenna: These are beach bags filled with things like sunscreen, sunglasses, flip-flops, and other fun things for the beach. Each guest gets a bag with their name on it.

Kyle: That's a good idea! And they look great.

Jenna: Thanks. It's a lot of work!

Kyle: Yeah, but Annie will be really happy.

Jenna: I hope so!

Kyle: So, what happens at a baby shower? I've never been to one.

Jenna: I think it depends on the shower, but usually someone close to the mother-to-be, like her sister or best friend, plans a party. There's food and games and sometimes the mom-to-be opens gifts.

Kyle: What kind of games do you play?

Jenna: There are a lot of different games. In one popular game you can't say the word "baby" at the party. When guests arrive, everyone is given a diaper pin and they wear it on their shirt. If one guest hears another guest say "baby," he or she can take the rule breaker's pin. The person with the most pins wins the game.

Kyle: That's kind of funny.

Jenna: Yeah. There are other games too like dirty diapers.

Kyle: Umm, what?

Jenna: Ha ha. The diapers aren't *actually* "dirty." You put melted chocolate bars inside diapers and everyone passes the diapers around and guesses what kind of candy bar it is?

Kyle: Wow. That's... interesting.

Jenna: It is. But it's fun!

Kyle: Well, I hope you have fun at the party! And I'm sure everyone will love the beach bags.

Jenna: Thanks!

83

양복점에서
-
AT THE TAILOR (B1)

저스틴: 안녕하세요. 바지 단을 올리고 싶은데요. 조금 길어서요. 그리고 이 셔츠 허리 쪽도 조금 좁게 줄이고 싶어요.

재단사: 좋아요. 바지와 셔츠를 입어 보시겠어요?

저스틴: 네, 그렇게 할게요.

재단사: 좋습니다, 탈의실은 바로 그쪽에 있어요.

저스틴: 감사합니다.

(삼 분 후...)

재단사: 좋아요, 거울 앞에 서 보세요. 자, 바지를 일 인치 줄이면 이 정도 길이가 될 거예요. 어때요?

저스틴: 네, 괜찮아 보여요.

재단사: 좋네요. 셔츠 한 번 봅시다.

저스틴: 허리가 약간 큰 것 같아요. 줄일 수 있을까요?

재단사: 물론이죠. 이건 어때 보여요?

저스틴: 흠... 좀 너무 딱 붙는 것 같아요. 조금 헐렁하게 할 수 있을까요?

재단사: 네. 어떠세요?

저스틴: 완벽해요.

재단사: 좋네요! 가셔서 옷 갈아입으세요. 셔츠와 바지에 핀이 꼽혀 있으니 벗을 때 조심하세요!

저스틴: 오, 알려 주셔서 감사합니다! 찔리고 싶지 않거든요!

재단사: 네, 찔리면 안 되죠!

(사 분 후...)

저스틴: 결제를 지금 하나요 아니면 나중에 하나요?

재단사: 고객님 원하시는 대로 해 주세요!

저스틴: 알겠습니다, 제가 옷을 찾아갈 때 결제를 할게요.

재단사: 좋아요.

저스틴: 언제 될까요?

재단사: 칠 일에서 십 일 정도 걸릴 것 같아요. 마무리되면 전화 드리겠습니다.

저스틴: 좋아요, 감사합니다.

재단사: 별 말씀을요. 좋은 하루 보내세요!

저스틴: 재단사 님도 좋은 하루 보내세요!

AT THE TAILOR

Justin: Hi. I'd like to get these pants hemmed. They're a little long. And I also want to make this shirt a little narrower on the sides.

Tailor: Great. Would you like to try on the pants and shirt?

Justin: Yes, please.

Tailor: All right, the fitting room is right there.

Justin: Thanks.

(Three minutes later...)

Tailor: Okay, come stand in front of the mirror. So, if I shorten them about an inch, they will be this long. How does that look?

Justin: Yeah, that looks good.

Tailor: Good. Let's take a look at the shirt.

Justin: I feel like it's a little wide on the sides. Can we take it in?

Tailor: Sure. How does this look?

Justin: Hmm... I actually think that's a little too tight. Can we make it a little looser?

Tailor: Yep. How's that?

Justin: That's perfect.

Tailor: Great! Go ahead and get changed. Be careful taking off your pants and shirt because there are pins in there!

Justin: Oh, thanks for the warning! I don't want to get jabbed!

Tailor: No, that wouldn't be good!

(Four minutes later...)

Justin: Do I pay now or later?

Tailor: It's up to you!

Justin: Okay, I'll pay when I pick them up.

Tailor: Sounds good.

Justin: When will they be ready?

Tailor: I think these will take between seven and ten days. I will give you a call when they're finished.

Justin: Great, thanks.

Tailor: No problem. Have a good day!

Justin: Same to you.

84

주차 공간 찾기

-

LOOKING FOR A PARKING SPOT (B1)

대니: 이 창고형 클럽은 힝싱 하루 중 이 시간이 제일 바빠. 우리 여기에 왜 또 온거야?

존: 글쎄, 우리는 북쪽에서 오는 친구들이랑 가족들과 함께 큰 파티를 할 거야. 사람이 많아서 물건을 대량으로 구매해야 돈을 아낄 수 있어. 게다가, 난 다른 날에는 시간이 없고.

대니: 핫도그랑 피자 먹으러 잠시 들를 수 없을까? 여기 피자 정말 맛있어.

존: 물론이지! 내가 너를 내려 주고, 주차할 곳을 찾는 동안 네가 주문을 하면 되겠다.

대니: 바보 같은 소리 마. 그냥 같이 주차 할 곳을 찾아보자. 어쨌든 주차가 오래 걸릴 것 같아.

존: 알았어. 저쪽 구석에 주차 공간이 보이는 것 같아!

대니: 여기서 돌아! 주차장에서 이 구역이 보통 차가 적더라고.

존: 좋은 생각이야! 아, 여기 공간이 있어—이봐!

대니: 저 사람이 방금 우리 자리를 훔친 거야? 분명히 우리 거였다고!

존: 나빴어.

대니: 아, 계속 찾아보자. 어! 하나 보이는 것 같아! 잠깐만... 차 불을 켜두고 나간 거구나. 차 안에는 아무도 없네.

존: 우리 지금 십오 분째 이 주차장을 돌고 있어. 큰 실수를 한 것 같은 기분이야.

대니: 너는 포기를 너무 쉽게 해... 저기 좀 봐! 저 사람 나간다!

존: 맞아! 이 자리는 우리 거야!

대니: 앗싸! 피자 먹자!

LOOKING FOR A PARKING SPOT

Dany: This warehouse club is always so busy at this time of day. Why are we here again?

Jon: Well, we have that giant party where all our friends and family from up north are coming down. With that many people, we need to purchase things in bulk quantities so we can save money. Plus, I don't have time any other day.

Dany: Can we at least stop for hot dogs and some pizza? Their pizza is awesome.

Jon: Sure! Maybe I should drop you off so you can order while I go find parking?

Dany: Don't be silly. Let's just look for a spot together. I feel like this is going to take much too long anyway.

Jon: Okay. I think I see a space in the far corner!

Dany: Turn in here! There are usually fewer cars in this section of the parking lot.

Jon: Good idea! Oh, here's a spot—HEY!

Dany: Did he just steal our parking space?! It was clearly ours!

Jon: That wasn't very nice.

Dany: Ugh, let's just keep looking. Oh! I think I see one! Oh wait... this person just left the car's lights on. There's no one in it.

Jon: We've been circling this parking lot for fifteen minutes now. I feel like I've made a huge mistake.

Dany: You give up too easily... look over there! That person is leaving!

Jon: Yes! This parking space is ours!

Dany: Hooray! Time for pizza!

85

뭘 볼까?

-

WHAT SHOULD WE WATCH? (B1)

윌: 오늘 밤에 놀러 가고 싶어?

칼라: 사실, 집에서 배달 음식 시켜 먹고, 스트리밍 서비스 하나 켜서 뭐 좀 보면 되겠다 생각했어.

윌: 좋네. 어짜피 나도 그닥 밖에 나가고 싶지는 않아. 태국 음식 시켜 먹는 거 어때?

칼라: 맛있겠다! 근데 더 중요한 건 뭘 보느냐는 거야.

윌: 좋은 질문이야. 남자가 비밀 정부 기관에 쫓기는 시리즈 마저 볼래?

칼라: 아니, 긴장감 넘치는 건 별로 안 당기네.

윌: 알았어, 영국에서 하는 베이킹 쇼는 어때?

칼라: 그 쇼 정말 좋은데, 오늘 밤에는 별로 안 보고 싶어.

윌: 알았어... 형사들이 오래된 범죄를 해결하는 그 쇼는 어때?

칼라: 흠, 알았어! 괜찮은 생각이야.

윌: 우리가 마지막으로 본 에피소드가 뭐였지?

칼라: 기억이 안 나.

윌: 형사들이 노스캐롤라이나에 있는 숲 속에 있었던 것 같은데?

칼라: 응! 네 말이 맞아! 네 번째 에피소드였던 거 같은데?

윌: 오와, 기억력 좋네. 다섯 번째 에피소드를 보자!

WHAT SHOULD WE WATCH?

Will: Do you want to go out tonight?

Kala: Actually, I was thinking we could stay at home, watch something on one of our streaming services, and get food delivered.

Will: That sounds great. I don't really feel like going out anyway. How does Thai food sound?

Kala: That sounds delicious! But more importantly, what should we watch?

Will: Good question. Do you want to finish watching that series where that guy is being chased by some secret government agency?

Kala: Nah, I don't feel like watching something suspenseful.

Will: Okay, how about that baking show from England?

Kala: I love that show but I don't feel like watching it tonight.

Will: All right... how about that show where the detectives are trying to solve old crimes?

Kala: Hmm, okay! That sounds good.

Will: What was the last episode we watched?

Kala: I can't remember.

Will: I think they were in a forest in North Carolina?

Kala: Yes! You're right! That was episode four, I think?

Will: Wow, good memory. Let's watch episode five!

86

호텔 체크인하기

-

CHECKING IN AT THE HOTEL (B1)

안내원: 안녕하세요. 호텔 바이 더 씨에 오신 것을 환영합니다. 무엇을 도와 드릴까요?

프레디: 안녕하세요, 존스라는 성으로 예약했어요.

안내원: 좋습니다, 제가 한 번 찾아볼게요. 네... 킹 베드가 있는 큰 방이 삼 박 예약되어 있네요.

프레디: 맞습니다.

안내원: 신분증과 예약할 때 사용하셨던 신용카드를 볼 수 있을까요?

프레디: 네, 여기 있습니다.

안내원: 감사합니다. 어디에서 오셨나요?

프레디: 저희는 베이 지역에서 왔어요.

안내원: 아, 멋지네요! 베이 지역 참 좋아해요.

프레디: 마찬가지예요! 저희는 샌디에이고도 정말 좋아해서 일 년에 한 번씩 오려고 해요.

안내원: 저도 샌디에이고 좋아해요! 그래서 여기 살고 있죠. 어쨌든, 돌아오신 걸 환영합니다!

프레디: 감사합니다! 실은, 전망 보이는 방이 있나요?

안내원: 확인해볼게요. 오, 운이 좋으시네요! 전망 보이는 방 하나가 오 분 전에 취소되었어요!

프레디: 우와! 여쭤보길 잘 했네요.

안내원: 저도 그렇게 생각해요! 컴퓨터에 고객님의 정보를 수정할게요.

프레디: 네, 기다릴게요.

안내원: 좋습니다... 이제 다 됐어요. 이건 열쇠고 이건 와이파이 정보입니다. 저기 모퉁이를 돌면 엘리베이터가 있어요.

프레디: 좋습니다, 감사합니다!

안내원: 천만에요. 즐겁게 지내시고 궁금한 점 있으시면 저희에게 알려 주세요.

프레디: 감사합니다!

CHECKING IN AT THE HOTEL

Receptionist: Hello. Welcome to Hotel by the Sea. How can I help you?

Freddy: Hi, we have a reservation under the last name Jones.

Receptionist: Great, let me look that up. Okay... you have a large room with a king bed for three nights.

Freddy: Yes.

Receptionist: Can I see your ID and the credit card you used to make the booking?

Freddy: Yes, here they are.

Receptionist: Thank you. So where are you traveling from?

Freddy: We're from the Bay Area.

Receptionist: Oh, nice! I love the Bay Area.

Freddy: We do too! But we also love San Diego. We try to come here once a year.

Receptionist: I love San Diego too! That's why I live here. Well, welcome back!

Freddy: Thanks! Actually, are there any rooms with views available?

Receptionist: Let me check. Oh, it looks like you're in luck! We had a cancellation about five minutes ago!

Freddy: Wow! I'm glad I asked.

Receptionist: I am too! Let me change your information in the computer.

Freddy: That's fine; I can wait.

Receptionist: All right... you're good to go. Here are your keys and this is the Wi-Fi information. The elevators are around the corner there.

Freddy: Great, thank you!

Receptionist: My pleasure. Enjoy your stay and please let us know if you have any questions.

Freddy: Thank you!

87

교수님께 말씀드려야만 해
-
YOU SHOULD TALK TO THE PROFESSOR (B1)

데비: 내가 이 수업을 잘 하고 있는 것 같지가 않아.

필: 진짜? 왜? 수업이 어려워?

데비: 응, 좀 어렵긴 하지만, 내가 일을 많이 해서 공부를 원하는 만큼 못 하겠더라고. 과제랑 시험 공부를 할 시간이 하루에 약 한 시간뿐이야. 한 세 시간 정도 필요한데 말이야!

필: 아, 그렇구나. 유감이네.

데비: 이 수업에서 점수를 잘 받아야 하기도 하고. 그래서 조금 걱정돼.

필: 일을 좀 덜 할 수는 없어?

데비: 지금은 안 돼. 가족을 도와야 해.

필: 알겠어. 교수님께 얘기해서 과제 제출까지 시간을 조금 더 주실 수 있는지 알아보는 건 어때?

데비: 그렇게 할까 생각 중이야. 하지만 교수님들께서는 학생들이 기간을 늘려달라 요청하는 것을 달가워 하시지 않아. 수업에 등록하는 게 교수님과 약속을 하는 거고, 또 그걸 진지하게 받아들여야 하니까.

필: 알아. 하지만 교수님께서 이해하실지도 모르지.

데비: 그래... 내일 교수님 근무 시간에 말씀드리러 가야겠어.

필: 어떻게 되어 가는지 나한테 알려줘.

데비: 그렇게 할게.

(다음날.)

데비: 그래서, 교수님께 말씀드렸어.

필: 그래? 어떻게 됐어?

데비: 교수님께서 정말 친절하셨어. 이번 주랑 다음 주에 숙제 기간을 연장해 주신데. 정말 감사해.

필: 정말 친절하시다. 봤지? 내가 말씀드리라고 했잖아!

데비: 알아. 여쭤보는 것이 그다지 마음에 편하지는 않았지만, 여쭤봐서 다행이야.

필: 음, 이 주 후에는 네 스케쥴이 진정되서 모두 균형이 잡히길 바랄게.

데비: 그랬음 좋겠어!

YOU SHOULD TALK TO THE PROFESSOR

Debbie: I don't think I'm doing very well in this class.

Phil: Really? Why? Is the class difficult?

Debbie: Yes, it's a little difficult, but I've been working a lot and I haven't been able to study as much as I would like. I only have about one hour a night to do homework and study for tests. I need about three hours!

Phil: Oh, I see. That's too bad.

Debbie: I need to get a good grade in this class, too. So, I'm a little worried.

Phil: Can you work a little less?

Debbie: Not right now. I need to help my family.

Phil: I understand. Maybe you can talk to the professor and see if he can give you a little extra time to finish assignments?

Debbie: I've been thinking about doing that. But professors don't like it when students ask for extensions. When you enroll in a class, that's a commitment you make and you have to take it seriously.

Phil: I know. But you never know. The professor may be understanding.

Debbie: Yeah... I think I'll go talk to him during his office hours tomorrow.

Phil: Let me know how it goes.

Debbie: I will.

(The next day.)

Debbie: So, I talked to the professor.

Phil: Yeah? How did it go?

Debbie: He was really nice. He's giving me an extension on the homework this week and next week. I'm so grateful.

Phil: That's so nice of him. See? I told you to talk to him!

Debbie: I know. I felt so bad for asking, but I'm glad I did.

Phil: Well, hopefully after a couple weeks your schedule will calm down and you'll have time to balance everything.

Debbie: I hope so!

88

배낭여행 계획하기

-

PLANNING A BACKPACKING TRIP (B1)

자넷: 우리 여행 계획을 시작해야 해!

카를로스: 응, 그래야 해! 지금 시간 있어?

자넷: 응. 앉아서 노트북이랑 여행 책을 같이 보자.

카를로스: 알았어, 나는 커피를 좀 끓일게.

자넷: 좋아. 예산부터 결정해야 할 것 같아.

카를로스: 맞아.

자넷: 삼천오백 달러 어때?

카를로스: 각각 삼천오백 달러, 아니면 둘이 합쳐서?

자넷: 음, 당연히 둘이 합쳐서지!

카를로스: 알았어, 좋아. 걱정했잖아!

자넷: 우리가 바르셀로나로 가는 비행기를 탄다면 표 하나에 왕복 천 달러 정도야.

카를로스: 흠... 그럼 천오백 달러 정도 남겠네. 너는 며칠 동안 일을 쉴 수 있어?

자넷: 십 일. 너는 이 주 정도 쉴 수 있지, 그렇지?

카를로스: 응.

자넷: 그럼, 가는 날과 오는 날을 제외하고 두 번의 주말을 포함하면 유럽에서 십이 박을 보낼 수 있어.

카를로스: 좋아. 십이 박에 천오백 달러가 있다는 거네. 너는 어떤 나라에 가고 싶어?

자넷: 글쎄, 우리는 바르셀로나로 가면 스페인에서 시간을 보낼 수 있을 거야. 스페인 외에도 이탈리아랑 프랑스에도 정말 가고 싶어.

카를로스: 포르투갈은 어때? 나는 꼭 거기에 가고 싶어. 스페인과도 가깝잖아.

자넷: 십이 박에 사 개국은 너무 많은 걸까?

카를로스: 음, 우리는 각 장소에서 이틀 혹은 삼일 밤만 보낼 수 있겠어.

자넷: 삼 개국만 가는 게 좋을 것 같아. 그러면 우리가 각 나라에서 시간을 조금 더 보낼 수 있을 거야.

카를로스: 알았어. 이탈리아는 다음에 갈까? 어차피 거기서는 더 오래 있고 싶거든.

자넷: 응, 이탈리아에 정말 가고 싶어 죽겠지만 그건 좋은 생각이야. 내가 부자여서 일을 하지 않아도 된다면 몰라도!

카를로스: 맞아, 그렇지? 그럼, 이제 우리 여행 일정을 생각해보자...

PLANNING A BACKPACKING TRIP

Janet: We need to start planning our trip!

Carlos: Yes, we do! Do you have time now?

Janet: Yep. Let's sit down with the laptop and our travel books.

Carlos: Okay, I'll make some coffee.

Janet: Great. I think we should start by deciding on a budget.

Carlos: I agree.

Janet: How does $3,500 sound?

Carlos: $3,500 each or for both of us?

Janet: Umm, definitely for both of us!

Carlos: All right, good. I was worried!

Janet: If we fly to Barcelona, the flight will be around $1,000 roundtrip for each ticket.

Carlos: Hmm… so then we will have around $1,500 left. How many days can you take off work?

Janet: Ten days. You can take two weeks off, right?

Carlos: Yeah.

Janet: So, with weekends and the flights there and back we can spend about twelve nights in Europe.

Carlos: Awesome. That means we have $1,500 for twelve nights. What countries do you want to go to?

Janet: Well, we're flying into Barcelona, so we can spend some time in Spain. Aside from Spain, I really want to go to Italy and France.

Carlos: What about Portugal? I really want to go there and it's close to Spain.

Janet: Do you think four countries in twelve nights is too much?

Carlos: Well, we would only be able to spend about two or three nights in each place.

Janet: I think we should just do three countries. Then we could spend a little more time in each country.

Carlos: Okay. What about if we saved Italy for another time? I really want to spend more time there anyway.

Janet: Yeah, I'm dying to go to Italy but I think that's a good idea. If only I were rich and didn't have to work!

Carlos: I know, right? Well, for now let's figure out our itinerary...

89

기념품 사기

-

BUYING SOUVENIRS (B1)

다니엘: 우리가 친구들이랑 가족들한테 줄 기념품을 사야 한다는 거 잊지마.

켄지: 응, 잊지 않았어. 한두 군데 상점만 가면 안 될까?길게 쇼핑하고 싶지 않아. 휴가가 이틀 밖에 남지 않았거든.

다니엘: 응, 두 시간 안에 전부 사도록 하자.

켄지: 알았어! 어디로 가야 할까?

다니엘: 중앙 시장에 가자. 거기서 음식과 토산품들을 팔아. 그리고 흥정도 할 수도 있어.

켄지: 그런데 넌 흥정을 할 줄 알아? 나는 잘 못 해!

다니엘: 넌 너무 착해! 좀 더 단호해져야 해. 원하는 가격으로 주지 않을 때는 자리를 떠야 해.

켄지: 해 볼게!

다니엘: 사라는 무엇을 사줘야 할까?

켄지: 커피 어때? 아니면 초콜릿. 아니면 둘 다.

다니엘: 좋은 생각이야. 사라가 커피를 좋아하지.

켄지: 아키히로는?

다니엘: 흠... 걔 선물은 고르기가 너무 어려워. 이미 모든 걸 갖고 있잖아!

켄지: 알아. 걔는 음식을 좋아해. 현지 간식을 사다 주면 되겠다.

다니엘: 맞아. 좋아, 간식으로 하자.

켄지: 그리고 너희 엄마는?

다니엘: 엄마는 집에 둘 예술 작품같은 걸 좋아하실 것 같아. 그림이나 소묘 같은?

켄지: 좋은 결정이야. 하지만 집으로 가져가는 게 어려울 거 같은데?

다니엘: 응. 여행 가방에 넣어도 망가지지 않는 걸 찾아야 해.

켄지: 맞아. 좋았어, 출발!

BUYING SOUVENIRS

Danielle: Remember, we still need to buy some souvenirs for our friends and family.

Kenji: Yep, I haven't forgotten. Can we go to just one or two stores? I don't want to spend too long shopping. We only have two more days left of our vacation.

Danielle: Yeah, let's try to buy everything in two hours.

Kenji: Okay! Where should we go?

Danielle: Let's go to the central market. They have food and local products. And you can bargain there.

Kenji: Can you do the bargaining, though? I'm not good at it!

Danielle: You're too nice! You have to be firmer. And you have to walk away if they don't give you the price you want.

Kenji: I'll try!

Danielle: What should we get Sarah?

Kenji: Maybe some coffee? Or chocolates. Or both.

Danielle: That's a good idea. She loves coffee.

Kenji: What about Akihiro?

Danielle: Hmm... it's so difficult to get presents for him. He already has everything!

Kenji: I know. He likes food. We could get him some local snacks.

Danielle: True. Okay, snacks it is.

Kenji: And how about your mom?

Danielle: I think she would love some kind of art for her house. Maybe a painting or drawing?

Kenji: Good call. But will it be hard to transport it home?

Danielle: Yeah. We need to find something that won't get ruined in our suitcases.

Kenji: Right. Okay, off we go!

90

직업 변경

-

CAREER CHANGE (B1)

자라: 직장을 그만둘 생각이야.

티제이: 진짜?! 왜? 네 일을 좋아하는 줄 알았어!

자라: 예전에는 좋아했는데 좀 지루해졌어.

티제이: 무슨 말이야?

자라: 매일 똑같은 일을 하는 것 같아. 좀 더 도전적인 걸 하고 싶어.

티제이: 알겠다. 그럴 수 있지.같은 분야에 일을 찾아볼 거야 아니면 완전 다른 분야로 찾아 볼 거야?

자라: 모르겠어. 회계가 좋긴 하지만 사실 인테리어 디자인 쪽으로 해 볼까 생각 중이야.

티제이: 정말?! 우와, 큰 변화겠다. 어쨌든 난 네가 인테리어 디자인을 정말 잘할 것 같아.

자라: 고마워! 너도 알다시피, 내가 항상 취미로 인테리어 디자인에 관심이 있었지만 이걸 직업으로 하면 어떨지 고민해 왔었어.

티제이: 정말 흥미로운 소식이야! 어떤 종류의 인테리어 디자인인지 생각해 봤어?

자라: 아직 확실하진 않은데 레스토랑 디자인을 돕고 싶긴 해.

티제이: 오, 그건 재미있겠다. 네가 회계에서 그랬던 것처럼 인테리어도 지겨워할 것 같아?

자라: 그렇게 생각하지 않아. 인테리어는 창의력이 필요하고 항상 다른 걸 디자인하잖아.

티제이: 그래, 말이 되네. 그럼, 이 새로운 여정에 행운을 빌어!

자라: 고마워! 어떻게 되어 가는지 알려 줄게.

CAREER CHANGE

Zara: I think I'm going to quit my job.

T.J.: Really?! Why? I thought you loved your job!

Zara: I used to love it, but I've gotten kind of bored.

T.J.: What do you mean?

Zara: I feel like I do the same thing every day. I want something a little more challenging.

T.J.: I see. That makes sense. Are you going to look for a job in the same field or in a totally different field?

Zara: I don't know. I like accounting but I'm actually thinking of getting into interior design.

T.J.: Really?! Wow, that would be a big change. I think you'd be so good at interior design, though.

Zara: Thanks! As you know, I've always been interested in it as a hobby. But I've been thinking about pursuing it as a career.

T.J.: This is such interesting news! Any ideas about what kind of interior design?

Zara: I'm not sure yet. I'd love to help design restaurants though.

T.J.: Oh, that would be fun. Do you think you'd get bored with interior design like you have with accounting?

Zara: I don't think so. It requires creativity, and you're always designing something different.

T.J.: Yeah, that makes sense. Well, good luck on this new journey!

Zara: Thanks! I'll keep you updated.

91

은퇴 파티 계획하기

-

PLANNING A RETIREMENT PARTY (B1)

트리쉬: 안녕하세요, 개릿 씨. 우리는 빌 씨의 은퇴 파티 계획을 세워야 해요. 빌 씨의 마지막 날은 오늘부터 한 달 뒤 거든요.

개릿: 네, 거기에 대해서 이야기 나눠 봐요! 지금 잠깐 시간 있으세요?

트리쉬: 네. 제가 적을 수 있도록 펜이랑 종이를 가져 올게요.

개릿: 알겠어요.

트리쉬: 그래서, 어떻게 생각하세요? 파티는 사무실에서 할까요, 아니면 레스토랑 같은 곳에서 할까요?

개릿: 제 생각에 사무실은 너무 좁은 것 같아요. 그리고 빌 씨가 이십오 년 동안 여기 계셨으니까 사무실 밖에서 축하를 해야 할 것 같아요.

트리쉬: 동의해요. 모두 다 즐길 수 있을 거예요. 또, 빌의 가족들도 원하시면 오셔도 되고요.

개릿: 네.

트리쉬: 새로운 레스토랑 허스가 괜찮다고 이야기를 많이 들었어요. 들어본 적 있으신가요?

개릿: 네, 들어봤어요! 저도 가보고 싶었어요.

트리쉬: 저도요. 예약이 가능한 이벤트 방이 레스토랑 뒤쪽에 있어요. 온라인에서 그 방이 얼마나 하는지 봅시다.

개릿: 네.

트리쉬: 아, 가격이 그렇게 나쁘지는 않네요. 세 시간에 삼백 달러예요.

개릿: 그렇게 근사한 레스토랑인데 가격이 괜찮네요.

트리쉬: 네. 흠... 파티는 무슨 요일에 해야 할까요?

개릿: 팔월 오일 금요일 어때요?

트리쉬: 완벽한 것 같아요.

개릿: 좋아요! 레스토랑에서 음식을 제공하나요?

트리쉬: 아마 음료와 전채 요리를 제공할 거예요.

개릿: 좋습니다, 식당에 물어볼 질문 몇 가지를 적어 놓을게요. 그날에 모두 올 수 있는지 물어봐 주시겠어요?

트리쉬: 물론이죠!

PLANNING A RETIREMENT PARTY

Trish: Hey, Garrett. We should start planning Bill's retirement party. His last day is a month from today.

Garrett: Yes, let's talk about it! Do you have a few minutes now?

Trish: Yeah. Let me go get a pen and paper so I can take some notes.

Garrett: Okay.

Trish: So, what do you think? Should we have the party at the office or somewhere else, like a restaurant?

Garrett: I think the office is too small. And he's been here twenty-five years. I feel like that calls for an out-of-the-office celebration.

Trish: I agree. I think that would be more enjoyable for everyone. And that way Bill's family can come if they want.

Garrett: Yep.

Trish: I've heard great things around that new restaurant Hearth. Have you heard of it?

Garrett: Yeah, I have! I've been meaning to try it.

Trish: Me too. They have a room in the back that you can reserve for events. Let's look online and see how much it is.

Garrett: Okay.

Trish: Oh, the price isn't that bad. It's $300 for a three-hour event.

Garrett: That sounds good for such a nice restaurant.

Trish: Yeah. Hmm... what day should we have the party?

Garrett: What about Friday, August 5?

Trish: I think that's perfect.

Garrett: Great! Does the restaurant provide food?

Trish: They probably provide some drinks and appetizers.

Garrett: All right, I'll write down some questions to ask the restaurant. Do you want to ask everyone if they can make it that day?

Trish: Sure!

92

제 여행 가방이 나오지 않았어요

-

MY SUITCASE DIDN'T SHOW UP (B1)

리나: 안녕하세요. 삼십 분 기다렸는데 제 여행 가방이 아직 나오지 않았어요.

쿠엔틴: 비행기 번호가 뭐였나요?

리나: LK145 요.

쿠엔틴: 알겠습니다, 제가 찾아 볼게요. 흠... 네, 가방이 다 나왔을 텐데요. 이 사무실 앞에 있는 짐은 확인해 보셨나요?

리나: 네.

쿠엔틴: 알겠습니다, 불편을 끼쳐 죄송합니다. 분실한 가방 보고서를 작성해 주세요. 고객님의 가방은 다음 비행기에 실렸거나 덴버에서 오는 비행기에서 아예 실리지 않았거나 두 가지 중에 하나예요.

리나: 으윽. 알겠습니다. 여기 오는 데 며칠 걸릴 것 같나요?

쿠엔틴: 이르면 오늘 저녁에 도착할 수도 있지만, 내일 도착할 가능성도 있어요. 내일 저녁까지는 도착할 거예요.

리나: 그 가방 안에 일과 관련한 중요한 서류가 있어요. 이 상황이 썩 유쾌하지는 않네요.

쿠엔틴: 다시 한 번 불편을 끼쳐 죄송합니다. 가능한 빨리 가방을 받기 위해서 저희가 할 수 있는 모든 일을 하겠습니다.

리나: 감사합니다. 제가 공항에 가방을 찾으러 와야 하는 건가요?

쿠엔틴: 집에 누군가가 계시면 고객님 집 주소로 가방을 배달해 드릴 수 있습니다.

리나: 오늘 밤에는 제가 집에 있을 거고 내일은 제 남편이 있을 거예요.

쿠엔틴: 완벽해요. 집에 아무도 안 계시면 저희가 가방을 다시

공항으로 가져올 거예요. 그럼 이곳에서 가방을 찾을 수 있으실 거예요. 아니면 다음 날 다시 가방을 배달해 드릴 수도 있습니다.

리나: 누군가는 집에 있을 거예요.

쿠엔틴: 좋습니다. 다시 한 번 고객님의 가방이 지연된 점에 대해 사과드립니다. 좋은 하루 보내세요.

리나: 감사합니다. 좋은 하루 보내세요.

MY SUITCASE DIDN'T SHOW UP

Rina: Hi. I've been waiting for thirty minutes and my suitcase still hasn't come out.

Quentin: What was your flight number?

Rina: LK145.

Quentin: OKAY, let me look that up. Hmm... yes, all of the bags should be out. Have you checked the luggage in front of this office?

Rina: Yes.

Quentin: Okay, I apologize for the inconvenience. Please fill out this missing bag report. Your bag was either put on a later flight, or it never made it on the flight from Denver.

Rina: Ugh. I see. How many days do you think it'll take to get here?

Quentin: It may get here as early as this evening, but it's possible it could get here tomorrow. I think it should arrive by the end of the day tomorrow.

Rina: I have some important documents for work in that bag. I'm not very happy about this.

Quentin: Again, I'm sorry for the inconvenience, ma'am. We'll do everything we can to get your bag back to you as soon as possible.

Rina: Thanks. Do I have to come back to the airport to pick it up?

Quentin: We can deliver it to your address if someone will be home.

Rina: I'll be home tonight and my husband will be home tomorrow.

Quentin: Perfect. If no one is home, we'll bring it back to the airport and you can pick it up here. Or we can try to deliver it again the next day.

Rina: Someone should be home.

Quentin: Sounds good. Again, I apologize that your bag has been delayed. Have a good day.

Rina: Thanks. Same to you.

93

팁 주는 관습

-

TIPPING CUSTOMS (B1)

제이콥: 아직도 여기서 팁을 주는 게 익숙하지 않아. 덴마크에서는 팁을 거의 안 주거든.

엘라: 정말?

제이콥: 응. 덴마크에서는 서비스 요금이 계산서에 포함되어 있어. 팁을 줘도 되는데, 반드시 그래야 하는 건 아니야.

엘라: 아, 그렇구나. 팁이 판매세처럼 여기 계산서에 포함되어 있으면 좋겠어. 나는 수학을 잘 못해서 팁을 계산하는 데 너무 오래 걸리거든!

제이콥: 하하, 진짜? 그냥 휴대폰에 있는 계산기 사용하면 돼.

엘라: 알아. 때로는 쉽지만 서너 명씩 계산서를 나눌 때는 어려워.

제이콥: 맞아.

엘라: 유럽에서는 팁을 주는 게 흔해?

제이콥: 어디에서 어떤 종류의 서비스를 받느냐에 따라 달라져. 대부분이 선택 사항이야. 만약 팁을 얼마나 줘야 할지 모르겠다면 십 퍼센트 정도 주는 게 좋고. 하지만 서비스가 나쁘면, 팁을 줄 필요가 전혀 없어.

엘라: 그게 훨씬 더 쉬울 것 같아.

제이콥: 응, 그리고 아이슬란드와 스위스에서는 팁을 전혀 주지 않아도 돼.

엘라: 알아두면 좋은 정보야.

제이콥: 그리고 독일에서는 종업원에게 네가 얼마를 낼 건지 알려줘야 해. 그러니까, 너의 계산서가 이십 유로인데 이 유로의 팁을 주고 싶어. 그래서 이십오 유로를 건넨다고 치면 종업원에게 "이십이 유로"라고 말하는 거지. 그러면, 종업원이 너에게 삼 유로를 돌려 줄 거야.

엘라: 그렇구나. 우와, 너는 팁에 대해서 많이 알고 있구나!

제이콥: 하하. 음, 여행을 많이 다녔어.

엘라: 운이 좋네!

TIPPING CUSTOMS

Jakob: I still can't get used to tipping here. We rarely tip in Denmark.

Ella: Really?

Jakob: Yeah. In Denmark service charges are included in the bill. You can tip, but you don't have to.

Ella: Oh, I see. I wish tipping was included in the bill here, like sales tax. I'm not good at math and it takes me forever to calculate the tip!

Jakob: Ha ha, really? You can just use the calculator on your phone.

Ella: I know. Sometimes it's easy, but it's harder when you're splitting the bill with three or four people.

Jakob: True.

Ella: Is tipping common in Europe?

Jakob: It depends on where you are and what kind of service you're getting. It's mostly optional. If you're not sure how much to tip, you should tip around 10 percent. But if the service is bad, you don't have to tip anything.

Ella: That sounds much easier.

Jakob: Yeah, and in Iceland and Switzerland you don't need to tip at all.

Ella: That's good to know.

Jakob: And in Germany you should tell the server how much to charge you when you're paying the bill. So, if your bill is twenty euros and you want to tip two euros, you hand him, say, twenty-five euros, and you tell him "twenty-two euros." Then, he will give you three euros back.

Ella: I see. Wow, you know a lot about tipping!

Jakob: Ha ha. Well, I've kind of traveled a lot.

Ella: Lucky guy!

94

미술관 여행

-

TRIP TO THE ART MUSEUM (B1)

리사: 우리가 여기에 오다니! 이 전시회를 보게 돼서 기뻐. 나는 항상 십팔 세기의 일본 그림을 좋아했거든.

마크: 일본 미술은 어떻게 알게 된거야?

Lisa: 대학교에서 미술 역사 수업을 들었는데 특히나 십팔 세기부터의 일본 미술에 끌렸어. 우키요에라고 불리는 스타일이 아주 멋있어.

Mark: 흥미롭네. 음, 네가 그것에 대해서 내게 가르쳐 줄 수 있을지도 몰라!

Lisa: 그러고 싶어!

Mark: 전시회로 들어가는 입구는 여기야.

Lisa: 야호!

Mark: 아, 여기 있는 그림을 봐봐. 색이 굉장해.

Lisa: 응, 나는 우키요에 그림의 밝은 색들을 정말 좋아해.

Mark: 왜 그림이 모두 비슷하게 생긴 거야?

Lisa: 그게 그 당시의 스타일이었어.

Mark: 그리고 게이샤 그림이 엄청 많아.

Lisa: 응, 게이샤는 인기 있는 주제였어.

Mark: 풍경화도 정말 멋져.

Lisa: 그렇지? 난 그 시기의 풍경화가 너무 좋아. 그러는 너는 어떤 종류의 미술을 좋아해?

Mark: 음, 모르겠어. 미술에 대해 생각해 본 적이 없거든. 나는 사진을 좋아해.

Lisa: 정말? 어떤 종류의 사진?

Mark: 흑백 사진, 초상화...

Lisa: 흥미롭네. 너 사진도 찍어?

Mark: 가끔! 잘하지는 못해. 실은 수업도 듣고 싶고 최종적으로 멋진 카메라에 투자하고 싶어.

Lisa: 그러면 좋겠다! 그렇게 해 봐.

Mark: 생각 중이야.

Lisa: 이제 우리 이 층에 있는 전시를 보러 갈까?

Mark: 그래!

TRIP TO THE ART MUSEUM

Lisa: We're here! I'm excited to see this exhibit. I've always liked eighteenth-century Japanese paintings.

Mark: How did you discover Japanese art?

Lisa: I took an art history class in college and I've been drawn to Japanese art ever since, especially from the eighteenth century. There's a style called Ukiyo-e that's very cool.

Mark: Interesting. Well, maybe you can teach me about it!

Lisa: I'd love to!

Mark: Here is the entrance to the exhibit.

Lisa: Yay!

Mark: Oh, look at this painting here. The colors are awesome.

Lisa: Yeah, I love the bright colors of Ukiyo-e paintings.

Mark: Why do all the paintings look so similar?

Lisa: That was the style back then.

Mark: And there are so many paintings of geishas.

Lisa: Yeah, that was a popular subject.

Mark: The landscape paintings are really cool, too.

Lisa: Aren't they? I love the landscapes from that period. So, what kind of art do you like?

Mark: Umm, I don't know. I've never really thought about it. I like photography.

Lisa: Really? What kind of photography?

Mark: Black and white photos, portraits...

Lisa: Interesting. Do you take pictures?

Mark: Sometimes! I'm not very good. I'd like to take a class, actually, and eventually I want to invest in a nice camera.

Lisa: That would be great! You should.

Mark: I'm thinking about it.

Lisa: Should we go see the exhibit on the second floor now?

Mark: Sure!

95

정전
-
POWER OUTAGE (B1)

엘리자베스: 내 생각에 전기가 나간 것 같아.

정우: 정말? 난 네가 불을 끈 줄 알았어.

엘리자베스: 아니야. 화장실 불을 켜 봐.

정우: 안 켜져.

엘리자베스: 침실 불은?

정우: 안돼. 켜지지 않아.

엘리자베스: 흠, 알았어.

정우: 아, 방금 전기 회사에서 문자를 받았어. 전기가 한 시간 동안 들어오지 않을 거래.

엘리자베스: 아, 알았어. 나쁘진 않네. 촛불을 켤 시간이야!

정우: 우리한테 양초가 많아서 다행이야. 로맨틱한 저녁을 먹을 수 있겠어!

엘리자베스: 하하. 응, 그럴 수 있지! 아, 존한테서 방금 문자가 왔는데 걔네 집도 전기가 나갔대.

정우: 아, 정말?

엘리자베스: 응. 놀랍네. 존은 삼 마일 떨어진 곳에 살거든!

정우: 무슨 일이 있었던 건지 궁금해.

엘리자베스: 모르겠네. 저녁은 준비가 됐어! 우리가 뭘 먹는지 볼 수 있도록 탁자 위에 촛불 두어 개를 더 놓자.

정우: 좋은 생각이야! 오늘 밤에 더이상 놀라고 싶지 않거든.

엘리자베스: 아, 방금 전기 회사한테서 문자를 받았어. 풍선이 전선에 닿아서 정전이 생긴 거라고 하네.

정우: 아 진짜?

엘리자베스: 전기가 최소 두 시간 동안 나갈 거라고도.

정우: 우와. 우리 디저트도 로맨틱하게 먹을 것 같네!

엘리자베스: 응, 그럴 것 같아!

POWER OUTAGE

Elizabeth: I think the power just went out.

Jung-woo: Really? I thought you just turned out the lights.

Elizabeth: No. Try turning on the bathroom light.

Jung-woo: It isn't working.

Elizabeth: What about the bedroom light?

Jung-woo: Nope. That's not working either.

Elizabeth: Hmm, okay.

Jung-woo: Oh, I just got a text from the electric company. It says that the power will be out for an hour.

Elizabeth: Ugh, all right. That's not too bad. It's time to light the candles!

Jung-woo: It's good that we have a lot of candles. We can have a romantic dinner!

Elizabeth: Ha ha. Yes we can! Oh, John just texted me. He said the power is out at his house, too.

Jung-woo: Oh, really?

Elizabeth: Yeah. I'm surprised. He lives three miles away!

Jung-woo: I wonder what happened.

Elizabeth: I don't know. But dinner is ready! Let's put a couple more candles on the table so we can see what we're eating.

Jung-woo: Good idea! We don't need any more surprises tonight.

Elizabeth: Oh, I just got a text from the electric company. It says the power outage was caused by balloons touching the power lines.

Jung-woo: Oh really?

Elizabeth: It also says the power will be out for at least two hours.

Jung-woo: Wow. I guess we will have a romantic dessert too!

Elizabeth: Yep, I guess so!

96

소셜 미디어를 얼마나 자주 사용하세요?

-

HOW OFTEN DO YOU USE SOCIAL MEDIA? (B1)

마르티나: 안녕하세요, 줄리안 씨.

줄리안: 안녕하세요, 마르티나 씨!

마르티나: 뭐하고 계세요?

줄리안: 그냥 제 소셜 미디어 피드를 보고 있었어요.

마르티나: 소셜 미디어를 얼마나 자주 사용하세요?

줄리안: 음, 모르겠어요. 아마 하루에 두 시간에서 세 시간 정도요? 마르티나 씨는 어때요?

마르티나: 아마 거의 비슷할 거예요.

줄리안: 이건 정말 시간 낭비예요!

마르티나: 그렇게 생각하세요? 때로 시간 낭비라고 여기다가도 가끔은 이게 사람들에게 정말로 가치 있다고 생각해요.

줄리안: 무슨 뜻인가요?

마르티나: 글쎄요, 저는 소셜 미디어가 친구나 가족과 계속 연락할 수 있는 편리한 방법이라고 생각해요. 소셜 미디어는 우리에게 새로운 소식을 알려 주고, 다른 나라와 문화에 대해 배울 수 있게 해줘요.

줄리안: 네, 저는 소셜 미디어가 사람들과 계속 연결될 수 있도록 도와주고, 최근 시사 문제를 놓치지 않도록 한다는 데에는 동의해요. 하지만 다른 문화를 배우는 데에 소셜 미디어가 우리에게 어떤 도움을 주나요?

마르티나: 제가 다른 나라의 여행 사진작가와 작가들을 팔로우하거든요. 그래서 그분들의 사진과 캡션으로 다른 장소에 대해 배울 수 있더라고요.

줄리안: 아, 그렇군요. 맞아요, 그건 좋은 점이에요. 소셜미디어가 많은 장점이 있다고 생각하지만 해로울 수도 있다고도 생각해요. 많은 사람들이 대부분 자신의 삶이 멋지게 보이는 사진을 올리지만, 완벽한 삶을 가진 사람은 없거든요. 그리고 그런 사진을 보는 몇몇 사람들이 자신들의 삶에 대해 안 좋게 생각할 수 있고요.

마르티나: 저는 그 부분에 전적으로 동의해요. 소셜 미디어는 확실히 사람들을 불안하고 시기하도록 만들 수 있어요. 대부분이 그렇듯이, 소셜 미디어도 적당히 해야 좋아요!

HOW OFTEN DO YOU USE SOCIAL MEDIA?

Martina: Hey, Julian.

Julian: Hey, Martina!

Martina: What are you doing?

Julian: Just scrolling through my social media feeds.

Martina: How often do you use social media?

Julian: Oh, I don't know. Maybe two or three hours a day? What about you?

Martina: Probably about the same.

Julian: It's such a waste of time!

Martina: You think? Sometimes I think it's a waste of time, but other times I think it's really valuable to people.

Julian: What do you mean?

Martina: Well, I think social media is a convenient way to keep in touch with friends and family, it gives us a way to follow the news, and it enables us to learn about other countries and cultures.

Julian: Yeah, I agree that it helps us stay connected with people and make sure we're up-to-date on current events. But how does it help us learn about other cultures?

Martina: I follow a lot of travel photographers and writers from other countries, so I can learn about different places from their photos and captions.

Julian: Oh, I see. Yeah, that's a good thing. I think social media has a lot of benefits, but I think it can also be harmful. Many people post photos that make their lives look amazing, but no one has a perfect life. And seeing those photos can make some people feel bad about their own lives.

Martina: I totally agree with that. Social media can definitely make people insecure and jealous. Like most things, social media is good in moderation!

97

면접 준비하기

-

PREPARING FOR A JOB INTERVIEW (B1)

앨리: 나 다음 주에 면접이 있는 데 너무 긴장돼!

나단: 진짜? 어떤 면접인데?

앨리: 의류 매장의 매니저 자리 면접이야.

나단: 우와 매니저! 잘됐네. 너가 소매업에서 오래 일을 했으니 확실히 다음 단계로 갈 시간이야!

앨리: 응, 그런 것 같아. 나는 새로운 도전을 할 준비가 됐어. 높은 급여를 받을 준비도 되었고.

나단: 하하, 그것도 좋겠다! 그래서 이 일은 어떻게 찾은 거야?

앨리: 온라인에서 찾았어. 일을 찾기 시작하고 몇 주 밖에 되지 않았어. 지난주에 이 일의 채용 공고를 보고 이력서랑 자기소개서를 보냈거든. 그리고 이틀 후에 연락이 왔어.

나단: 굉장히 빠르다! 네 이력서가 정말 인상적인가 봐.

앨리: 와, 고마워. 열심히 했지!

나단: 그래서, 면접에서 네게 어떤 걸 물어볼 거라고 생각해?

앨리: 아마도 고객 서비스에서 일했던 경험이랑, 직장에서 맞닥뜨린 어려움, 그리고 그걸 어떻게 극복했는 지에 대해서 물어볼 거 같아. 아마 내게 몇 가지 시나리오를 주고서 내가 어떻게 처리할 건지 물어볼 것 같아. 그런 모든 대답을 연습하고 있어.

나단: 좋네. 넌 잘 해낼 거야.

앨리: 모르겠어. 내가 면접에서 긴장을 많이 하거든.

나단: 그건 정상이야. 너 자신을 믿기만 하면 돼. 네가 이미 그 일을 하고 있다고 상상해봐.

앨리: 헤헤, 알았어. 그렇게 할게!

나단: 인터뷰 어떻게 되어 가는지 내게 알려줘!

앨리: 그럴게!

PREPARING FOR A JOB INTERVIEW

Allie: I have a job interview next week and I'm so nervous!

Nathan: Oh really? What's the interview for?

Allie: It's for a manager position at a clothing store.

Nathan: Oh wow, manager! Good for you. You've been working in retail for so long; it's definitely time for the next step!

Allie: Yeah, I think so. I'm ready for a new challenge. And a higher salary.

Nathan: Ha ha, that would be nice too! So how did you find out about this job?

Allie: Online. I've only been looking at jobs for a couple weeks. I found this job posting last week and sent them my resume and cover letter. They got back to me two days later.

Nathan: That's pretty quick! You do have an impressive resume.

Allie: Aww, thanks. I've worked hard!

Nathan: So, what do you think they're going to ask you?

Allie: Probably about my experience working in customer service, difficulties I've encountered on the job and how I've overcome them. They may give me a couple scenarios and then have me tell them what I would do. I've been practicing all of those answers.

Nathan: That's good. I think you'll do great.

Allie: I don't know. I get really nervous in interviews.

Nathan: That's normal. You just have to believe in yourself! Imagine that you already have the job.

Allie: He-he, okay. I'll do that!

Nathan: Let me know how the interview goes!

Allie: I will!

98

세탁소로 가는 길

-

TRIP TO THE DRY CLEANERS (B1)

앨리스: 좋은 아침입니다. 안녕하세요?

슈오웬: 네, 안녕하세요?

앨리스: 네.

슈오웬: 이거 맡기고 싶어요.

앨리스: 알겠습니다. 저희 시스템에서 계정을 조회할 건데 전화번호를 제게 말씀해 주시겠어요?

슈오웬: 여기에 처음 와봐요.

앨리스: 그렇군요. 전화번호, 그리고 이름과 성을 알려 주시겠어요?

슈오웬: 네. 제 이름은 슈오웬이고 성은 첸 입니다.

앨리스: 이름 철자가 어떻게 되세요?

슈오웬: "snake"의 "S", "happy" 의 "h", "under"의 "u", "octopus"의 "o", 그리고 "water"의 "w", "elephant"의 "e", 그리고 "Nebraska"의 "n"입니다.

앨리스: 감사합니다.

슈오웬: 여기에 와인 얼룩이 있어요. 얼룩을 제거할 수 있을까요?

앨리스: 항상 그렇듯이 저희가 최선을 다하겠습니다. 알려 주셔서 감사합니다.

슈오웬: 그리고 이 세탁소에서 독한 화학 물질을 사용하시나요?

앨리스: 아니요, 저희 세탁소가 친환경적이라는 점에서 자부심이 있습니다.

슈오웬: 그래서 여기가 다른 곳들보다 조금 더 비싼가요?

앨리스: 네, 맞습니다. 저희는 환경과 고객의 건강을 보호하고자 합니다.

슈오웬: 알겠습니다. 좋네요.

앨리스: 여기 영수증입니다. 옷은 금요일 오후 한 시에 준비될 것입니다.

슈오웬: 좋아요, 감사합니다!

앨리스: 감사합니다! 좋은 하루 보내세요.

TRIP TO THE DRY CLEANERS

Alice: Good morning. How are you?

Shuo wen: I'm good, thanks. How are you?

Alice: I'm good. Thanks for asking.

Shuo wen: I would like to drop these off.

Alice: Okay. Could you tell me your phone number so I can look up your account in our system?

Shuo wen: This is my first time here.

Alice: I see. Can I have your phone number and your first and last name?

Shuo wen: Yes. My first name is Shuo wen and my last name is Chen.

Alice: How do you spell your first name?

Shuo wen: "S" as in "snake," "h" as in "happy," "u" as in "under," "o" as in "octopus," and then "w" as in "water," "e" as in elephant, and "n" as in "Nebraska."

Alice: Thank you.

Shuo wen: There is a wine stain here. Do you think you can get that out?

Alice: We'll try our best, as always. Thank you for pointing that out.

Shuo wen: And do you guys use harsh chemicals at this dry cleaner?

Alice: No, we pride ourselves on being environmentally friendly here.

Shuo wen: Is that why you're a little more expensive than other places?

Alice: Yes, exactly. We want to protect the environment and our customers' health.

Shuo wen: I see. That's good.

Alice: Here is your receipt. These will be ready on Friday after 1 p.m.

Shuo wen: Great, thank you!

Alice: Thanks! Have a nice day.

99

좋아하는 날씨

-

FAVORITE KIND OF WEATHER (B1)

아만다: 너무 추워!

로버트: 난 이게 좋아.

아만다: 정말? 무슨 소리야? 추워 죽겠어!

로버트: 내겐 안 그래. 이건 내가 좋아하는 날씨야.

아만다: 넌 이상해.

로버트: 너는 어떤데? 너는 찌는 듯한 날씨만 좋아하잖아.

아만다: 하하, 나는 따뜻한 날씨를 좋아하는 거지 찌는 듯한 날씨는 아니야.

로버트: 넌 여름에 행복하겠지만 나는 여름을 견디는 게 힘들어.

아만다: 너는 시베리아로 이사해야 해.

로버트: 그거 좋겠어! 지루할 거라는 걸 빼면 말이야. 러시아어도 할 줄 모르고.

아만다: 알아, 그건 문제가 될 수도 있어.

로버트: 넌 데스 벨리로 이사해야만 해.

아만다: 거기가 어디야?

로버트: 캘리포니아에 있어.

아만다: 살기에 좋은 곳처럼 들리지는 않네.

로버트: 좋게 들리진 않지. 하지만 거기가 더운 곳이라 네가 좋아할 거야.

아만다: 여전히 그닥 매력적으로 들리지는 않는 걸.

로버트: 더워도 건조하면 괜찮은 데 덥고 습한 건 못 참겠더라고.

아만다: 응, 나도 약간의 습기는 감당할 수 있지만 많은 건 감당할 수 없어.

로버트: 우리가 작년에 플로리다에 갔을 때 기억해? 너무 습했어.

아만다: 맙소사. 그렇게 습한 곳에 가본 건 처음이었어!

로버트: 맞아! 조금도 밖에 있을 수가 없었어.

아만다: 맞아.

로버트: 음, 이제 아직 십이 월이라 다행이야. 추운 계절이 두어 달 정도 더 남았어.

아만다: 으윽, 나는 빨리 봄이 왔으면 좋겠어!

FAVORITE KIND OF WEATHER

Amanda: It's so cold!

Robert: I love it.

Amanda: Really? What are you talking about? It's freezing!

Robert: Not for me. This is my favorite kind of weather.

Amanda: You're weird.

Robert: What about you? You only like scorching weather.

Amanda: Ha ha, I like warm weather but not *scorching* weather.

Robert: You're so happy in the summer, but for me it's unbearable.

Amanda: You should move to Siberia.

Robert: I would love that! Except I'd probably get bored. And I don't speak Russian.

Amanda: Yeah, that might be a problem.

Robert: You should move to Death Valley.

Amanda: Where is that?

Robert: In California.

Amanda: That doesn't sound like a fun place to live.

Robert: No, it doesn't. But it's hot there, so you'd like it.

Amanda: It still doesn't sound very appealing.

Robert: Dry heat is okay, but I can't stand humidity.

Amanda: Yeah, I can handle a little humidity, but not a lot.

Robert: Do you remember when we went to Florida last year? It was so humid.

Amanda: Oh my gosh. I've never experienced anything like that!

Robert: I know! You couldn't even stay outside for more than a few minutes.

Amanda: Exactly.

Robert: Well, I'm glad it's only December. We get a couple more months of cold weather.

Amanda: Ugh, I can't wait for it to be spring!

100

빨래하기

-

DOING LAUNDRY (B1)

어제이: 우리는 네가 대학에 가기 전에 빨래하는 법을 가르쳐 줘야 해! 벌써 열일곱 살인데 제대로 빨래하는 법을 배운 적이 없다는 게 믿기지가 않아.

니샤: 나 빨래할 줄 알아요..

어제이: 응, 하지만 잘 못하잖아. 네가 너무 많은 옷을 망가트려 놓았어!

니샤: 몇 벌만 그랬죠.

어제이: 응, 내 옷 몇 벌! 세탁기에 흰색으로 들어가서 분홍색으로 나왔던 내 셔츠 기억해?

니샤: 분홍색이 잘 어울렸어요!

어제이: 나는 분홍색 셔츠를 원한게 아냐!

니샤: 알았어요. 죄송해요.

어제이: 괜찮아. 난 그 충격에서 회복했어. 하지만 네가 대학에 들어가서 더 많은 옷을 망가트리는 걸 원치 않아.

니샤: 저도요. 알겠어요, 그래서 우리 세탁 교육은 언제예요?

어제이: 지금 시간 좀 있어?

니샤: 네.

어제이: 알았어. 그러면, 우선 밝은 옷과 어두운 옷을 분리해야 해.

니샤: 뭐가 밝은거고 뭐가 어두운 거예요?

어제이: 밝은색은 하얀색, 베이지색, 회색, 하늘색... 그런 것들이야. 어두운색은 검은색, 갈색, 짙은 회색, 그리고 선명한 색.

니샤: 알겠어요. 물은 얼마나 뜨거워야 해요?

어제이: 어두운 옷이라면 찬물을 추천해. 밝은 옷이라면 따뜻한 물이나 뜨거운 물을 사용해도 되고.

니샤: 그리고 얼마나 오래 옷들을 세탁해야 해요?

어제이: 음, 우선 물 온도를 선택하고 이 버튼을 눌러. 그러고 나서 세탁 종류의 선택해. 난 보통 "일반"으로 해. 그리고 "시작" 버튼을 눌러. 정말 간단해.

니샤: 오, 정말 간단하네요. 제가 할 수 있을 것 같아요.

어제이: 나도 네가 할 수 있다고 생각해! 대학에 들어가면 네 옷은 네가 빨아도 괜찮아.

니샤: 하하. 절 믿어줘서 고마워요, 아빠!

DOING LAUNDRY

Ajay: We need to teach you how to do laundry before you go away to college! I can't believe you're already seventeen and you haven't learned how to do laundry properly.

Nisha: I know how to do laundry.

Ajay: Yes, but not well! You've ruined so many clothes!

Nisha: Only a few things.

Ajay: Yeah, a few of *my* things! Remember my shirt that went into the washing machine white and came out pink?

Nisha: It looked good pink!

Ajay: I didn't want a pink shirt!

Nisha: Okay. I'm sorry about that.

Ajay: It's fine. I've recovered from that trauma. But I don't want you to ruin any more clothes in college.

Nisha: Me neither. All right, so when is our laundry lesson?

Ajay: Do you have some time now?

Nisha: Sure.

Ajay: Okay. So, first you need to separate the dark clothes from the light clothes.

Nisha: What is "light" and what is "dark"?

Ajay: Light colors are white, beige, grey, light blue… things like that. Dark clothes are black, brown, dark grey, and bright colors.

Nisha: I see. How hot should the water be?

Ajay: For dark clothes, I recommend cold water. For light colors, you can use warm or hot water.

Nisha: And how long do I wash them for?

Ajay: Well, first you choose the water temperature and push this button. Then you choose the type of wash. I usually go with "regular." Then you push the "start" button. It's that easy.

Nisha: Oh, that is easy. I think I can do that.

Ajay: I think you can too! If you get into college, you can wash your own clothes!

Nisha: Ha ha. Thanks for believing in me, Dad!

101

작년 추수감사절

-

LAST YEAR'S THANKSGIVING (B1)

케이틀린: 안녕하세요, 그랜트 씨. 올해 추수 감사절에는 어떤 걸 할 거예요?

그랜트: 제 사촌 집에 갈 거예요. 제 부모님, 조부모님, 이모와 삼촌, 그리고 사촌 세 명이 거기 있을 거예요.

케이틀린: 우와! 꽤 큰 모임이네요.

그랜트: 네 그래요! 케이틀린 씨는 추수 감사절에 무엇을 하실 거예요?

케이틀린: 전 추수 감사절에 일을 해야 해요! 전 너무 우울해요!

그랜트: 오 이런! 진짜 별로네요!

케이틀린: 네, 그것이 요식업계에서 일하는 단점 중에 하나예요. 하지만 돈을 더 받으니 그건 좋아요.

그랜트: 그런 식으로 보상을 받을 수 있겠네요. 추수 감사절에는 주로 무엇을 하세요?

케이틀린: 저희는 보통 부모님 댁에 가서 저녁을 먹어요.

그랜트: 보통 어떤 걸 먹어요?

케이틀린: 속을 채운 칠면조와 호박파이요. 모두 평범한 추수감사절 음식이죠. 늘 맛있어요. 저희 가족에 훌륭한 요리사들이 많아요.

그랜트: 오, 멋지네요!

케이틀린: 네. 저는 작년에 으깬 감자를 꽤 맛있게 만들었어요. 제 자신이 너무 자랑스러웠어요! 제가 요리를 잘 못하거든요.

그랜트: 저도요! 근데 저는 먹는 건 좋아해요.

케이틀린: 저도요! 우리 가족은 늘 함께 카드놀이를 해요. 일종의 추수감사절 전통인 거죠. 작년에는 저녁 먹고 세 시간 동안 카드놀이를 했어요!

그랜트: 우와! 저녁을 먹은 후에 잠에 들지 않았다는 것이 놀랍네요! 저는 추수 감사절에 저녁을 먹고 나서는 늘 쓰러져서 자요.

케이틀린: 맞아요. 저도 놀랐어요! 우리는 게임에 푹 빠졌어요!

그랜트: 와, 그건 멋지네요. 그럼, 내년에 가족들과 추수 감사절을 보낼 수 있기를 바랄게요.

케이틀린: 저도요.

LAST YEAR'S THANKSGIVING

Caitlin: Hey, Grant. What are you doing for Thanksgiving this year?

Grant: I'm going to my cousin's house. My parents, grandparents, my aunt and uncle, and three of my cousins will be there.

Caitlin: Oh, wow! That's a pretty big gathering.

Grant: Yeah it is! What are you doing for Thanksgiving?

Caitlin: I have to work on Thanksgiving! I'm so bummed!

Grant: Oh no! That's terrible!

Caitlin: Yeah, that's one of the downsides of working in the restaurant industry. But I get paid more, so that's good.

Grant: That kind of makes up for it, I guess. What do you usually do for Thanksgiving?

Caitlin: We usually go to my parents' house and have dinner.

Grant: What do you guys usually eat?

Caitlin: Turkey and stuffing and pumpkin pie—all the usual Thanksgiving food. It's always delicious; we have a lot of great cooks in my family.

Grant: Oh, awesome!

Caitlin: Yeah. I made some pretty good mashed potatoes last year; I was proud of myself! I'm not a good cook.

Grant: Me neither! I love to eat, though.

Caitlin: Me too! My family always plays cards together too. It's kind of a Thanksgiving tradition for us. Last year we played for three hours after dinner!

Grant: Oh wow! I'm surprised you guys didn't fall asleep after dinner! I always pass out after dinner on Thanksgiving.

Caitlin: I know. I'm surprised too! We were so into the game!

Grant: Aww, that's cool. Well, I hope you can spend Thanksgiving with your family next year.

Caitlin: I do too.

102

몸이 좋지 않아

-

NOT FEELING WELL (B1)

엘리나: 안녕, 게리. 나는 오늘 집에 있을 것 같아. 몸이 좋지 않아.

게리: 오, 이런! 무슨 일이야?

엘리나: 머리가 아프고 어지러워. 토할 거 같아.

게리: 네가 먹은 것 때문이야? 식중독에 걸렸을지도 몰라.

엘리나: 모르겠어. 아침으로 오믈렛을, 점심으로 피자를, 그리고 저녁으로 스테이크를 먹었어.

게리: 특이한 것이 있는 것처럼 보이지는 않는데. 어제 뭐 했어?

엘리나: 음, 날씨가 너무 좋아서 햇볕을 쬐고 싶어서 해변에 갔어.

게리: 네가 햇볕을 너무 오래 쬐었나 봐.

엘리나: 하지만 난 밖에 한 시간만 있었어.

게리: 물 좀 마셨어?

엘리나: 별로.

게리: 온종일 물을 안 마셨어?

엘리나: 응...

게리: 너 아마 탈수된 것 같아.

엘리나: 그렇게 생각해?

게리: 아마도. 온종일 물을 마시지 않고 한 시간 동안 햇볕을 쬐면 탈수 상태가 될 수도 있어.

엘리나: 어떻게 해야 해?

게리: 실내에 머무르며 물을 마셔!

엘리나: 알았어.

NOT FEELING WELL

Elina: Hey, Gerry. I think I'm going to stay home today. I'm not feeling well.

Gerry: Oh, no! What's wrong?

Elina: I have a headache and I feel dizzy. I think I might throw up.

Gerry: Was it something you ate? You might have food poisoning.

Elina: I don't know. I had an omelet for breakfast, pizza for lunch, and a steak for dinner.

Gerry: That doesn't seem like anything unusual. What did you do yesterday?

Elina: Well, I went to the beach because it was such a nice day and I wanted to soak up some sun.

Gerry: Maybe you stayed out in the sun too long.

Elina: But I was only outside for an hour.

Gerry: Did you drink any water?

Elina: Not really.

Gerry: No water all day?

Elina: No...

Gerry: You're probably dehydrated.

Elina: You think?

Gerry: Maybe. If you don't drink water all day and then you stay in the sun for an hour, you can get dehydrated.

Elina: What should I do?

Gerry: Stay inside and drink water!

Elina: Okay.

103

스노보드 여행

-

SNOWBOARDING TRIP (B1)

사만다: 자, 조니, 처음으로 산에서 보드를 타고 내려갈 준비 됐니?

조니: 있잖아, 난 이게 좋은 생각인지 잘 모르겠어.

사만다: 넌 할 수 있을거야!

조니: 그래서, 이게 윈드 서핑 같은 건데, 파도 대신에 눈 위에서 하는 거 맞지?

사만다: 완전히 그렇지는 않아. 먼저 네가 알아야 할 정말 중요한 것이 몇 가지 있어.

조니: 이걸 지금 말해주는 거야?

사만다: 적어도 말은 해주는 거야!

조니: 알았어, 그럼 내가 알아야 할 정말 중요한 것이 뭐야?

사만다: 첫째로, 네 발이 보드에 연결되어 있다는 것을 기억해야 해.

조니: 알았어. 그건 너무 당연한 거지. 방향을 잡자고 보드 위를 걸을 수는 없지.

사만다: 네가 이해해서 기쁘네.

조니: 다음은 뭐야?

사만다: 보드 앞부분으로는 진짜로 방향을 잡을 수 없어. 보드 끝을 잡을 거고, 그럼 반드시 산 아래로 구르게 되는데 그건 별로 재미 없을 거야.

조니: 응, 재미 없을 거야!

사만다: 대신에, 어깨로 방향을 끌고 보드 뒷부분 끝을 이용해 회전해.

조니: 알았어. 또 다른 건?

사만다: 없어! 갈 시간이야!

조니: 알았어. 내가 먼저 갈까?

사만다: 응! 네가 아직 코스를 잘 모르겠지만, 표지판을 따라가면 괜찮을 거야. 내가 바로 네 뒤에 있을게.

조니: 알았어, 간다!

SNOWBOARDING TRIP

Samantha: So, Johnny, are you ready for your first ride down the mountain?

Johnny: You know, I'm not so sure this is a good idea.

Samantha: You'll be fine!

Johnny: So, this is just like surfing but instead of waves, it's on snow, right?

Samantha: Not quite. There are a few really important things you need to know first.

Johnny: You're telling me this now?

Samantha: At least I'm telling you!

Johnny: Okay, so what are these few really important things I need to know?

Samantha: First, you have to remember that your feet are connected to your board.

Johnny: Right. That's obvious. I can't walk the board to steer.

Samantha: I'm glad you understand.

Johnny: What's the next thing?

Samantha: You can't really steer with the front of your board. You'll catch an edge and surely tumble down the mountain. That wouldn't be very fun.

Johnny: No, it would not!

Samantha: Instead, lead with your shoulders and use the back end of your board to turn.

Johnny: Okay. Anything else?

Samantha: Nope! Time to go!

Johnny: All right. Should I go first?

Samantha: Sure! I know you don't really know the course yet, but just follow the signs and you should be fine. I will be right behind you.

Johnny: All right, here we go!

104

집을 페인트칠하기

-

PAINTING THE HOUSE (B1)

클라크: 거실을 무슨 색으로 칠하면 좋을까?

발렌티나: 초록색처럼 밝고 재미있는 색으로 칠해야 한다고 생각해.

클라크: 초록색? 어떤 초록색 계통?

발렌티나: 라임 녹색?

클라크: 라임?! 나는 회록색이나 황록색은 괜찮아. 근데 라임은 모르겠어. 회색 같은 건 어때?

발렌티나: 회색? 우울하게 들리는데.

클라크: 회색은 정말 깨끗하고 현대식으로 보여. 여기, 내가 사진 보여 줄게.

발렌티나: 흠... 그렇게 나빠 보이지는 않네. 회색빛을 띤 파란색은 어때?

클라크: 괜찮을 것 같아.

발렌티나: 이 사진을 봐. 이런 거.

클라크: 응, 꽤 맘에 드네.

발렌티나: 정말?

클라크: 응.

발렌티나: 우와, 우리는 여기에 동의하는 거야?

클라크: 그런 것 같아! 좋아, 그럼 페인트 색은 정했고, 용품을 사야 해.

발렌티나: 응, 사야 해. 페인트 롤러와 접시, 그리고 페인팅 붓 두 개가 필요해. 페인트 테이프도.

클라크: 우리 사다리도 필요하지, 맞지?

발렌티나: 응, 아담이 사다리를 빌려주기로 했어.

클라크: 아, 알았어. 완벽해.

발렌티나: 방이 좋아져야 할텐데!

클라크: 나도. 우리가 방 전체를 페인트칠 했는데 마음에 들지 않으면 어떡해?

발렌티나: 그건 우리가 감수해야 할 위험인 것 같아.

클라크: 응. 가게에 가서 용품을 구해 올까?

발렌티나: 좋아!

PAINTING THE HOUSE

Clark: What color should we paint the living room?

Valentina: I think we should paint it something bright and interesting, like green.

Clark: Green? What shade of green?

Valentina: Maybe a lime green?

Clark: Lime?! I could handle a sage green or a moss green. But I don't know about lime. What about some kind of grey?

Valentina: Grey? That sounds depressing.

Clark: Grey looks really clean and modern. Here, I'll show you pictures.

Valentina: Hmm... that doesn't look that bad. What about a greyish-blue color?

Clark: That might work.

Valentina: Look at this picture. Something like this.

Clark: Yeah, I kind of like that.

Valentina: Really?

Clark: Yeah.

Valentina: Wow, do we agree on this?

Clark: I think so! All right, so we've decided on the paint color. We need to buy some supplies too.

Valentina: Yes, we do. We need a paint roller and trays and a couple brushes. And some painter's tape.

Clark: We need a ladder too, right?

Valentina: Yeah, Adam is lending us his ladder.

Clark: Oh, okay. Perfect.

Valentina: I hope the room will look good!

Clark: Me too. What if we paint the whole room and then we don't like it?

Valentina: I guess that's a risk we have to take.

Clark: Yep. Want to go to the store and get the supplies?

Valentina: Sure!

105

아름다운 일몰

-

A BEAUTIFUL SUNSET (B1)

수산나: 오늘 산책하러 가자. 날씨가 진짜 좋은데 온종일 실내에서 꼼짝하지 않고 있었잖아.

폴: 좋은 생각이야. 블랙슨 해변에 있는 절벽으로 가면 좋을 것 같아. 일몰을 볼 수 있을 거야.

수산나: 알았어! 하지만 우리 바로 떠나야 해. 사십 분 후에 해가 질 거야.

폴: 알았어, 가자!

(가는 중...)

수산나: 그래서, 네가 봤던 것 중에 가장 아름다운 일몰은 뭐야?

폴: 흠... 태국에서 정말로 아름다운 일몰을 봤어.

수산나: 아 진짜? 그 일몰이 왜 아름다웠어?

폴: 오렌지, 핑크, 보라색과 같이 하늘에 멋진 색이 많이 있었어. 그리고 물론 태국의 해변에 있으면 모든 것이 훨씬 더 아름다워.

수산나: 응, 당연히 그렇겠지. 내가 언젠가 태국에 갈 수 있기를 바래.

폴: 난 정말 돌아가고 싶어. 아름다운 곳도 많고 사람들도 정말 친절해. 그리고 물론 음식도 정말 맛있고, 또 매우 저렴해!

수산나: 돈을 모으기 시작할 거야.

폴: 하하, 알았어!

수산나: 다 왔다! 제시간에 도착했어! 십 분 후면 해가 질 거야. 일몰 보기에 좋은 곳을 찾아보자.

폴: 저기 있는 바위는 어때?

수산나: 오, 좋아, 가자.

폴: 우와 정말 아름답다.

수산나: 태국만큼 아름다워?

폴: 거의! 좋은 생각이었어, 수산나. 우리 이런 걸 더 자주 해야 해.

수산나: 맞아. 적어도 한 달에 한 번은 일몰 보러 여기에 오자.

폴: 알았어!

A BEAUTIFUL SUNSET

Susana: Let's go for a walk today. It's such a beautiful day and we've been cooped up inside all day.

Paul: Good idea. We should go to the cliffs at Blackson Beach. We can catch the sunset there.

Susana: Okay! But we should leave soon. The sun is going to set in forty minutes.

Paul: Okay, let's go!

(On the way...)

Susana: So, what's the most beautiful sunset you've ever seen?

Paul: Hmm... I saw some really beautiful sunsets in Thailand.

Susana: Oh really? Why were they beautiful?

Paul: There were so many amazing colors in the sky—orange, pink, purple—and of course everything is a lot more beautiful when you're on a beach in Thailand!

Susana: Yeah, I bet. I hope I can go to Thailand someday!

Paul: I really want to go back. There were so many beautiful places and the people were so nice. And, of course, the food was amazing. And so cheap!

Susana: I'm going to start saving money.

Paul: Haha, okay!

Susana: We're here! We made it in time! The sun is going to set in ten minutes. Let's find a good spot to watch it.

Paul: What about that rock over there?

Susana: Oh, yes, let's go.

Paul: Wow, it's so beautiful.

Susana: As beautiful as Thailand?

Paul: Almost! This was a good idea, Susana. We should do this more often.

Susana: I agree. Let's come here to watch the sunset at least once a month!

Paul: Okay!

CONCLUSION

What a ride, huh? One hundred and five conversations in Korean, written for your learning and improvement of your grasp of the language! We hope that they've served to help give you a better understanding of conversational Korean and to provide you with a massive amount of learning material that most professors *won't* be providing you anytime soon!

We have one last round of tips for you, reader, now that you're done with the book and may suddenly be wondering what comes next:

1. **Study!** Nobody learns a new language overnight, and just skimming through this book once won't be enough for you to acquire the tools you've looked for. Re-read it, understand it and finally dominate it, and only then will you be truly learning.
2. **Rehearse!** Find a partner and rehearse or recreate the conversations that you see here. It'll work for your pronunciation and shake that shyness you may have!
3. **Create!** Take these conversations and make your own for other situations! There's always something you can produce on your own, and it'll help you improve your grasp of the tongue!
4. **Don't give up!** Giving up is for losers. Keep working and make your effort worth it. Results will come, trust us!

So, there we have it, readers, we've finally reached the end. We hope you enjoyed the book and continue to come back for more. We're certainly working hard to produce more books for you to improve your Korean. Take care and see you soon!

Good luck and don't quit! Success is always just a few steps away!

Thanks for reading!

MORE BOOKS BY LINGO MASTERY

Have you been trying to learn Korean and find yourself having trouble discovering and practicing new words?

Are traditional textbooks just not helping you out as you expected them to?

Do you think that there should be a better way to learning new words in any target language?

If you answered *"Yes!"* to at least one of those previous questions, then this book is for you! We've compiled the 2000 Most Common Words in Korean, a list of terms that will expand your vocabulary to levels previously unseen.

Did you know that — according to an important study — learning the top two thousand (2000) most frequently used words will enable you to understand up to 84% of all non-fiction and 86.1% of fiction literature and 92.7% of oral speech? Those are *amazing* stats, and this book will take you even further than those numbers!

In this book:

- A detailed introduction with tips and tricks on how to improve your learning - here, you will learn the basics to get you started on this marvelous list of Korean terms!

- A list of 2000 of the most common words in Korean and their translations
- An example sentence for each word – in both Korean *and* English
- Finally, a conclusion to make sure you've learned and supply you with a final list of tips

Don't look any further, we've got what you need right here!

In fact, we're ready to turn you into a Korean speaker... what are you waiting for?

Do you know what the hardest thing for a Korean learner is?

Finding PROPER reading material that they can handle...which is precisely the reason we've written this book!

You may have found the best teacher in town or the most incredible learning app around, but if you don't put all of that knowledge to practice, you'll soon forget everything you've obtained. This is why being engaged with interesting reading material can be so essential for somebody wishing to learn a new language.

Therefore, in this book we have compiled 20 easy-to-read, compelling and fun stories that will allow you to expand your vocabulary and give you the tools to improve your grasp of the wonderful Korean language.

How **Korean Short Stories for Beginners** works:

- Each chapter possesses a funny, interesting and/or thought-provoking story based on real-life situations, allowing you to learn a bit more about the Korean culture.
- Having trouble understanding Hangul? No problem – we provide you with the same story twice – one version fully in Korean and the other version with English translation added below each paragraph, allowing you to fully grasp what you are reading!

- The summaries follow a synopsis in Korean and in English of what you just read, both to review the lesson and for you to see if you understood what the tale was about.
- At the end of those summaries, you will be provided with a list of the most relevant vocabulary from that chapter, as well as slang and sayings that you may not have understood at first glance.
- Finally, you'll be provided with a set of tricky questions in Korean, giving you the chance to prove that you learned something in the story. Don't worry if you don't know the answer to any — we will provide them immediately after, but no cheating!

We want you to feel comfortable while learning Korean; after all, no language should be a barrier for you to travel around the world and expand your social circles!

So look no further! Pick up your copy of **Korean Short Stories for Beginners** and level up your Korean language skills *right now*!

Made in United States
Orlando, FL
04 December 2023

40172989R00186